Teaching Images of the Christian Faith

SYMBOLS
of Faith

For Intergenerational Use

Written by
Marcia Joslin Stoner

Designed by
Mark Foltz

Patterns by
Florence Davis

Cover Design by
Paige Easter

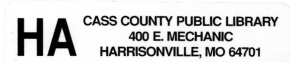

Abingdon Press

Symbols of Faith
Teaching Images of the Christian Faith
For Intergenerational Use

ISBN 0-687-09475-5

*A special thank you goes to Daphna Flegal, Dr. Gary Flegal, Marie Joslin,
and LeeDell Stickler for their help with craft directions.*

Art credits—pages 38 (nails), 41 (egg), 140-151: Charles Jakubowski;
page 108 (ship): Robert S. Jones; page 126: Brenda Gilliam;
pages 154-155: Randy Wollenmann.

01 02 03 04 05 06 07 08 09 10 — 10 9 8 7 6 5 4 3 2 1

Table of Contents

How to Use This Book

The symbols in this book have been separated into categories. However, keep in mind that in the life of the church symbols often have several meanings—so don't be afraid to combine or to pick and choose symbols from different sections.

FOR PRETEEN AND YOUTH ACTIVITIES

Information About Symbols—Let your students read about what different symbols of our faith represent.

Additional Activities—Need something extra to supplement a regular lesson? Pick out one or two activities that are appropriate to your subject, age group, and lesson needs.

Short-term Studies—Combine symbols and activities by categories and use the Lesson Plan Form on page 6 to quickly lay out a short-term study.

After-school-care or Youth Group Activities—Choose a symbol-related activity to do when you want to awaken interest or highlight a specific point with your group. Or, plan one or more sessions around the symbols of our faith.

FOR INTERGENERATIONAL ACTIVITIES

Third Grade Through Adult—Many activities in this book require an ability to read, so those in the third grade and up are best suited to appreciate the entire book. Let more sophisticated readers work with less sophisticated readers. You will find that some activities are most appropriate for the preteen level and beyond.

Kindergarten Through Adult—Choose mostly non-reading-oriented activities and let older children, youth, or adults help the younger children.

Preschool Through Adult—There are a few activities in this book that preschoolers can participate in (for example, playing musical instruments—they make a "joyful noise" better than any other group). Use photocopies of the symbols as coloring pages for the young ones or let them use modeling clay to shape their symbols.

FOR SHORT-TERM INTERGENERATIONAL STUDIES

Use the Lesson Plan Form on page 6 to set up short-term sessions for Advent, Lent, family retreats, a one-day Pentecost study—any event when it would be appropriate to learn about the symbols of the church. In this type of short-term study, try to form intergenerational groups that contain members of every age level. (Families may wish to work together; however, grouping different people of various ages together allows those without spouses or children an opportunity to participate more fully.)

FOR SPECIAL EVENTS or WORSHIP

Have a Banner Parade, set up a special altar, or make hot cross buns for a special event. Activities like these may take extra time to prepare, but the rewards will far outweigh the effort.

Sample Lesson Plan

This sample lesson plan is based on one possible way a class could use this book for a Lenten lesson. Making the Easter Timeline and working with the service project would require more than one session.

SESSION TIME: 2 hours

ARRIVAL ACTIVITY: Make a Bible Bookmark, p. 116
Supplies to gather: construction paper, markers, yarn, scissors, ruler, paper punch
Supplies to get / things to do: clear adhesive paper, dried flowers, make reduced-size photocopies of symbols

OPENING ACTIVITY: Research Symbols in the Bible, example on p. 116
Supplies to gather: Bibles, pencil, paper
Supplies to get / things to do: concordance (ask pastor), look up appropriate Bible passages

MAIN ACTIVITY: Holy Week Timeline, example on p. 42
Supplies to gather: Bibles, pencil, paper
Supplies to get / things to do: concordance (ask pastor), look up appropriate Bible passages

GAME: Symbols Concentration Game, p. 68
Supplies to gather: scissors, pen, glue
Supplies to get / things to do: make reduced-size photocopies of all Lenten/Easter symbols, buy index cards, make matching game

CRAFT: See opening activity, taken care of by Bible Bookmark
Supplies to gather: none
Supplies to get / things to do: none

MISSIONS: Serving With Others, p. 30 (this week–plan!)
Supplies to gather: information on several possible projects
Supplies to get / things to do: call Judy Johnson, mission chair, for help

MUSIC: Combine with worship
Supplies to gather: Tom Barton (make sure piano is in place for him)
Supplies to get / things to do: ask youth to carry hymnals from sanctuary to classroom

WORSHIP: Use reading on Jesus I found in my Upper Room magazine today
Supplies to gather: Upper Room magazine
Supplies to get / things to do: ask a preteen to lead the Lord's Prayer

What have I forgotten?

Lesson Plan Form

SESSION TIME

ARRIVAL ACTIVITY: _____
Supplies to gather: _____
Supplies to get / things to do: _____
_____

OPENING ACTIVITY: _____
Supplies to gather: _____
Supplies to get / things to do: _____
_____

MAIN ACTIVITY: _____
Supplies to gather: _____
Supplies to get / things to do: _____
_____

GAME: _____
Supplies to gather: _____
Supplies to get / things to do: _____
_____

CRAFT: _____
Supplies to gather: _____
Supplies to get / things to do: _____
_____

MISSIONS: _____
Supplies to gather: _____
Supplies to get / things to do: _____
_____

MUSIC: _____
Supplies to gather: _____
Supplies to get / things to do: _____
_____

WORSHIP: _____
Supplies to gather: _____
Supplies to get / things to do: _____
_____

What have I forgotten? _____
_____
_____

Symbols of Faith

Advent, Christmas, and Epiphany

Manger

The manger symbolizes the birth of Jesus. This symbol also suggests the ordinary life into which Jesus was born. A nimbus (halo) surrounding the manger indicates the presence of the holy child.

Activity: Move Your Nativity

Use your Nativity set to its full potential by gradually moving the different pieces of the display in the order listed below. This will help create a powerful visual impact by showing the events that led to Jesus' birth and the eventual visit of the wise men.

1. **A decree went out from Caesar Augustus.** Display the empty manger and place Mary and Joseph (and the donkey, if you have one) at a distance from the manger.

2. **There was no room in the inn.** Move Mary and Joseph into the crèche. Place the shepherds and sheep on a "hillside" at some distance from the manger.

3. **There were shepherds living in the fields, keeping watch over their flock by night.** Move the sheep and shepherds closer to the manger each time your group meets.

4. **You will find a child wrapped in bands of cloth and lying in a manger.** At the last meeting before Christmas, place baby Jesus in the manger.

5. At the first meeting after Christmas (or, if you will not meet for some time after Christmas, do this at the last meeting before Christmas), bring the sheep and shepherds into the crèche. Display the wise men and camels at a point somewhat distant from the crèche.

6. **We observed his star at its rising, and have come to pay him homage.** Start moving the sheep and the shepherds back toward their hill and move the wise men closer to the manger (or into the manger itself if your group meets on Epiphany, January 6).

7. **Get up, take the child and his mother, and flee to Egypt, for Herod is about to search for the child, to destroy him.** Start the wise men on a different route home and show Mary and Joseph heading out for Egypt.

How quickly the figures of the Nativity set are moved from one point to another will depend upon how often your group meets. If you use this activity at home with your family, you can move the Nativity figures daily. If you are doing this with a group that meets once a week or less, you will have to make a move every week or combine some of the moves.

Manger

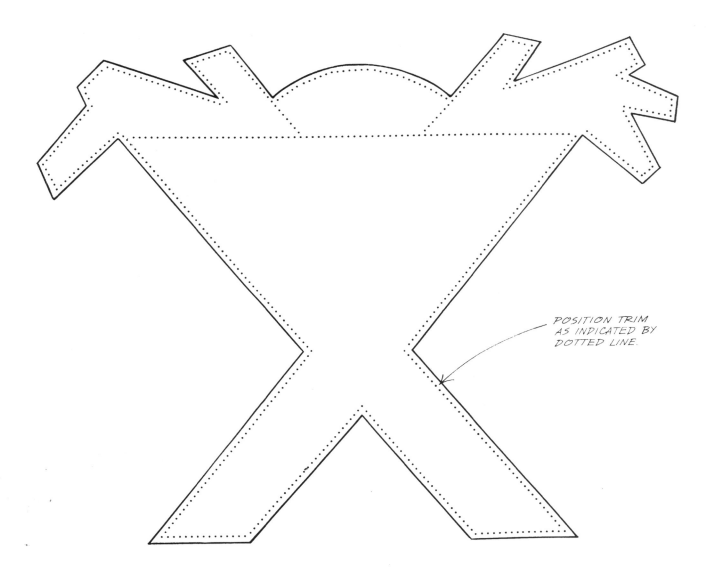

POSITION TRIM
AS INDICATED BY
DOTTED LINE.

Gifts of the Magi

Since there were three gifts—gold, frankincense, and myrrh—brought to the Christ Child, western legend has it that there were three wise men. Gold was considered valuable at the time of Jesus' birth for the same reasons it's considered valuable today. Frankincense and myrrh (Matthew 2:11) were used as incense. Frankincense was also used in medications. Myrrh was used in preparing bodies for burial. Both were considered appropriate gifts for a king.

Activity:
Throw a Christmas Baby Shower

Sponsor a baby shower for a local children's home, adoption agency, or homeless shelter as a symbol of the gifts that the wise men brought to Jesus. Check with agencies or shelters in your community to discover their needs. Make a list of these needs and set a time to deliver the gifts.

Have your group make "shower invitations" that show the date when all gifts must be collected. Be sure to indicate what types of gifts are needed and where they are to be collected.

Designate a centrally located "collection area," but make sure that it can be locked if the collection is to take place over more than one day. Placing the gifts under a Christmas tree or around a crèche can help to remind people of the reason why they are giving.

Set a time for your group to gather to get the gifts ready for delivery. You will need boxes or large garbage bags in which to put all the baby things. Don't forget to tag the boxes or bags as indicated by the receiving agency.

Deliver the gifts to the agency or shelter as a group. If you'd like, you could provide a little Christmas caroling for the workers of the organization. Be sure to include carols that deal with the baby Jesus, such as "Infant Holy, Infant Lowly," "Away in a Manger," "That Boy-Child of Mary," and so forth.

After delivering the presents, return to your church or starting point for hot chocolate and cookies and games. Have the group prepare a report for the congregation about how much was received and donated. This report could be done as an oversized "thank you" card to the congregation to be placed in a central area where all can see it, as an announcement after a worship service, or as a notice in your church newsletter.

Gifts of the Magi

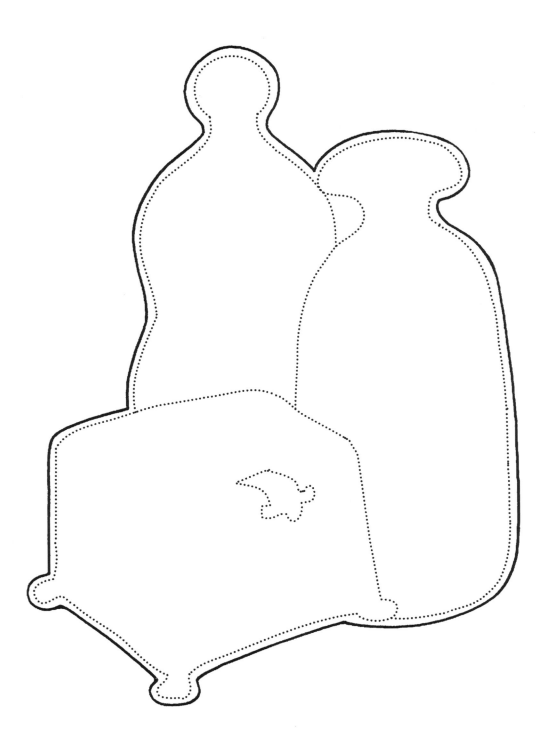

Angel

Angels are messengers of God and appear in both the Old and New Testaments. Art of angels often shows them with wings, which symbolizes their divine mission. Angels brought the news of Jesus' impending birth to both Mary and Joseph, and an angel was at the tomb of Jesus to announce the Resurrection (Matthew 28:1-10).

Activity: Mosaic Angels

Mosaics were created as far back as 4000 B.C. The earliest-known picture of Jesus is a mosaic that was made in the fourth century A.D. Mosaics were made of stone or ceramic, and present vivid symbols of the faith.

Group Mosaic

You will need:

- ¼" plywood cut into a square
- pencil
- photocopy of the angel symbol pattern (page 13)
- colored stones or small ceramic tiles
- sandpaper
- scissors
- craft or wood glue

Cut ¼" plywood into as large a square as you desire. Sand the wood.

Use a photocopy of the angel symbol pattern on page 13 (enlarged if desired) as a pattern for the mosaic. Outline the sections of the mosaic lightly in pencil. Then, in paint-by-number fashion, label the colors to be used in each section.

Let the groups work together over several weeks to fill in the spaces with colored stones or small ceramic tiles. Use a good quality craft or wood glue. Place the finished mosaic on display in a prominent area.

Individual Mosaics

You will need:

- cardboard, foamboard, or ¼" plywood cut into squares
- pencils
- copies of the angel symbol pattern (page 13)
- colored stones, small ceramic tiles, or colored foam sheets
- sandpaper
- scissors
- craft or wood glue

Cut cardboard, foamboard or ¼" plywood into 8" to 12" squares.

Ask each group member to
- Sand the square (if using wood).
- Trace the angel symbol pattern (page 13) onto the board, or draw an angel.
- Spread glue on ONE area of the picture at a time.
- Press stones, small ceramic tiles, or colored foam sheets (cut into small pieces) firmly onto the glue-covered area. To add colors and textures to the mosaics, sort the stones or tiles by color and use similar stones or ceramic tiles in the same areas.
- Let the mosaics dry completely before hanging them or turning them upright.

Stone pieces, ceramic tiles, foam sheets, and glue are available for purchase in your local craft store, or by calling S & S Worldwide at 1-800-243-9232.

Angel

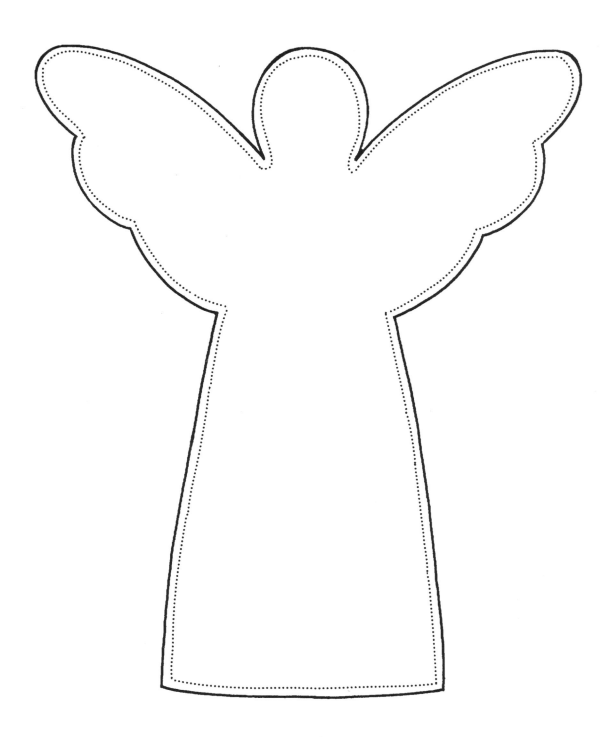

Star

The star is a powerful symbol for all peoples. For Christians the star symbolizes the promised coming of Christ. Stars can also represent God and the Holy Spirit, and the twelve-pointed star (see pages 118 and 119) can stand for the twelve disciples or the twelve tribes of Israel. The five-pointed star (shown here) is called the Star of Bethlehem or the Star of Epiphany. The word epiphany *means "showing forth." Epiphany is traditionally celebrated twelve days after Christmas, though in worship it is usually celebrated on the Sunday closest to the twelfth day after Christmas. The five-pointed star is not a Christmas symbol but an Epiphany symbol and is used in connection with the visit of the wise men, which reminds us of God's revelation of Godself to all the world in the Christ Child.*

Activity: A Galaxy of Stars

You will need:
  photocopies of the star pattern in various sizes (page 15)
  cardboard
  pencils
  scissors
  aluminum foil or gold or silver glitter paint and paintbrushes
  paper punch
  gold or silver braid

Photocopy the star pattern in various sizes and use these as templates for cutting out cardboard stars. Cover the cardboard stars in aluminum foil or paint them with gold or silver glitter paint. Punch a hole in the top point of each star, thread gold or silver braid through the hole (use different lengths of braid to create depth in your display), and hang the stars from the ceiling to make a spectacular display of a galaxy of stars.

Or, you could purchase ready-made three-dimensional cardboard stars from your local craft store and paint those stars with glitter paint.

These stars make a great "starry night" effect for a drama presentation, a party, or as decorations for any room for the Christmas season.

Star

POSITION TRIM
AS INDICATED BY
DOTTED LINE.

Symbols of Faith

Shepherd's Staff

The shepherd's staff is an ancient symbol for shepherds. Sheep (also lambs, see the General Christian Symbols section for more about symbols for sheep and lambs) and shepherds are often used as symbols in the Bible. God and Jesus are often referred to as "Shepherd." In the twenty-third Psalm we are told that "The Lord is my shepherd." Jesus told us that he was the "good shepherd" (John 10:11).

The candy cane was made in the shape of the shepherd's staff, specifically as a symbol of the humble shepherds who visited Jesus in Bethlehem. However, while the candy cane is strictly a Christmas symbol, the shepherd's staff is a year-round symbol of the shepherd as caretaker.

Activity: Christmas Symbol Cards

You will need:
  card stock and envelopes (available at craft stores)
  reduced-size photocopies of Christmas symbol patterns (your choice)
  pencils
  scissors
  stamps
  pens or felt-tip markers
  addresses
  sponges and paint or Christmas wrapping paper and glue or glitter pens

All of the following methods of making Christmas cards will use the card stock paper and reduced-size Christmas symbol patterns. (If you have time, go ahead and decorate the envelopes, too.)

1. Outline a symbol pattern lightly onto a sponge and cut the sponge around the traced shape. Dip the sponge in tempera paint and stamp the shapes onto the card. (It may help to dab the paint-soaked sponges onto paper towels first to soak up excess paint before touching them to the cards.)

2. Cut the symbol shapes out of old Christmas wrapping paper and glue them onto the card.

3. Place a symbol pattern on the card and trace around the pattern with a glitter pen.

Use any type of pen or marker to write a message on the inside of the card, and be sure to include an appropriate Bible message on the front, inside, or back of the card. Send these Christmas cards to homebound persons, missionaries, new people in the community, or anyone you know who might need to hear about the special meaning of Christmas.

Shepherd's Staff

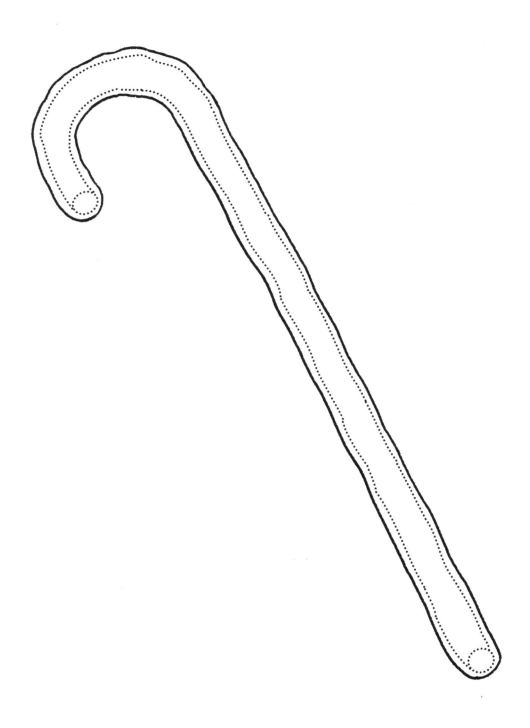

Symbols of Faith

Christmas Rose

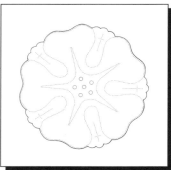

The Christmas Rose is a very hardy white rose that blooms at Christmastime. This rose is used as a symbol of the Nativity. It is also used as a symbol of messianic prophecy. Some Bible translations of Isaiah 35:1 use the word rose. *Others use the word* crocus *instead.*

Activity: Christmas Symbol Charades

You will need:
  reduced-size photocopies of Christmas symbol patterns
  small box or basket
  index cards (optional)

Make reduced-size photocopies of the Christmas symbol patterns in this book. (You may want to glue each symbol pattern copy to an index card. This way they will be sturdier and harder to see through.)

Fold the photocopies or cards in half, put them in a box or basket, and mix them up.

Divide the group into two teams. Let a representative of the first team draw (without looking) one of the symbols from the box or basket. This person must act out clues to help his or her teammates guess the symbol within a specified amount of time. (Since many of these symbols are relatively easy, you may want to limit the time to thirty seconds.) If the first team can't guess the symbol, let a representative of the second team act it out for his or her team members.

If the first team does guess correctly, give the second team a chance to draw a new symbol to act out. Keep reversing play between the teams until all the symbols have been guessed.

Note: Several other symbols from later parts of this book—such as the donkey, the lamb, the dove with an olive branch, the open Bible, or any of the symbols for Jesus—may also be used as Christmas symbols. You may want to photocopy these as well for use in the Christmas Symbol Charades activity.

Christmas Rose

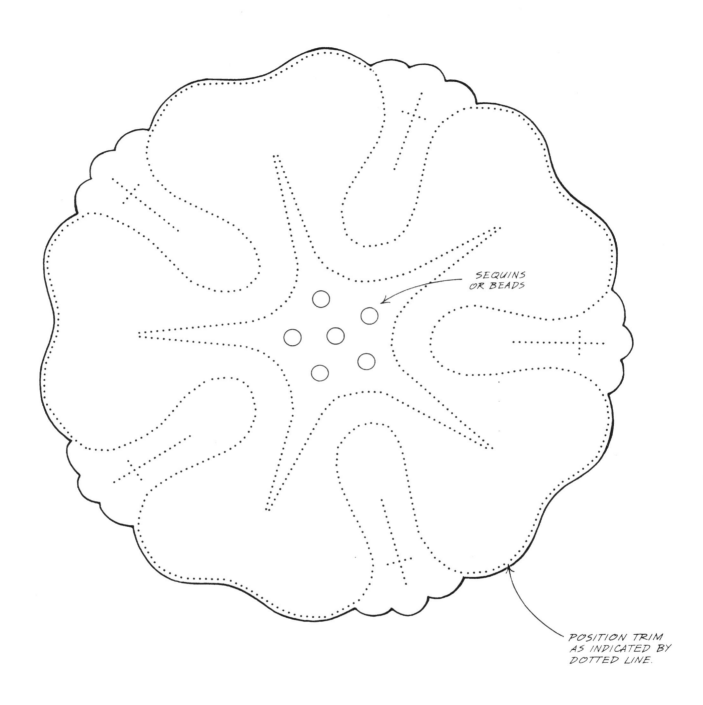

SEQUINS
OR BEADS

POSITION TRIM
AS INDICATED BY
DOTTED LINE.

Daisy

The daisy is a symbol of the innocence of the baby Jesus, the Holy Child, and was first used as a church symbol in the late fifteenth or early sixteenth century.

Activity: Symbols Relay Race

You will need:

Bibles	index cards	pencils
tape	small box or basket	

Write Bible references that pertain to each symbol you use on index cards (one Bible reference per card). Put these index cards in a small box or basket and place this on a table at one end of the room.

Divide your group into teams of four or five. Make sure each team has pencils and a Bible and have the teams stand on the other side of the room in single-file lines facing the table. Label an index card with each group's name ("Team 1," and so forth) and tape these cards to the table to designate where each group's cards will accumulate.

Give the following instructions:
At my signal, the first person on each team will run to the box (or basket) and take a card. The runner will take the card back to the team and hand it to the second person in line. The second person will look up the verse in the Bible and read it to the third person. The third person will write down the name of the symbol being talked about on the card and hand the card to the fourth person. The fourth person in line will write down what the symbol represents (either a person or a topic). Then that person (or, if you have five people on a team, pass the card to the fifth person) will run to the table and place the card on the team's designated spot. The runner then runs back to his or her place in line and the first person goes to the very end of the line. The person who was second in line in the first round now becomes the first person, and so forth.

Continue rotating assignments for several rounds. Then come back together as a group to check everyone's answers.

Some possible Bible references to use include

- Genesis 12:8-9—**tent**: Abraham
- Micah 7:14—**shepherd's staff**: shepherd, or the care the shepherd takes of sheep
- Matthew 2:1-2—**star**: Jesus' birth, the Epiphany
- Matthew 2:11—**three gifts**: wise men
- Matthew 3:11—**water**: baptism
- Matthew 26:26—**bread**: communion
- Matthew 26:27—**cup**: communion
- Luke 1:30—**angel**: God's messenger
- Luke 2:7—**manger**: Jesus' birth
- John 12:13—**palm branches**: Palm Sunday
- John 13:5—**towel and basin**: washing of the disciples' feet, servanthood
- Acts 2:3—**fire or flame**: Pentecost
- Revelation 22:13—**Alpha and Omega**: the Messiahship of Jesus Christ

There are many more. Use a concordance to find references for other symbols. (Note: Not all Christian symbols are based on the Bible; many come instead from centuries of tradition.)

Daisy

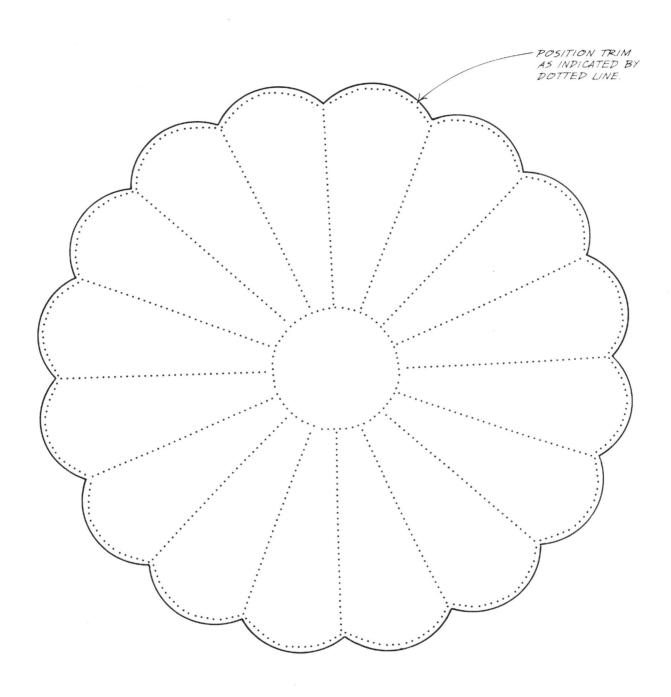

POSITION TRIM AS INDICATED BY DOTTED LINE.

Advent Wreath

The Advent wreath is full of symbolism. Its circular shape represents the unending love of God. The evergreens are used to represent eternal life. The four candles represent the four weeks of preparation before Christmas and are often purple, to represent Jesus' royalty. Sometimes one of the candles is pink, to represent either Mary, the mother of Jesus, or love. We add a white candle to the center of the Advent wreath on Christmas Eve or Christmas Day to represent Jesus. This candle is called the Christ candle.

Activity: Advent Worship

Advent is a time of preparation for the birth of Christ. The tradition of celebrating Advent started in France sometime around the fourth or fifth century.

One of the things we do most often in order to prepare for the birth of Christ is to light the Advent wreath. Take time each week to light a candle on the Advent wreath, read Scripture, and pray, either at home or in a church or classroom setting. Add your favorite Christmas music to make this Advent tradition even more special.

The different meanings of the four candles of the Advent wreath come from tradition only—they are not found anywhere in the Bible. Here is one list of candle meanings and suggested readings for your weekly Advent worship:

First week of Advent: Isaiah 11:6, "A little child shall lead them." The first candle stands for Christ our Hope.

Second week of Advent: Mark 1:2-4, "The voice of one crying out in the wilderness." The second candle symbolizes Christ the Way (or the prophets).

Third week of Advent: Luke 1:46-55, The Magnificat, or Mary's Song of Praise. The third candle represents Christ our Joy (or Mary, his mother).

Fourth week of Advent: Isaiah 9:6-7, "For a child has been born for us." The fourth candle is for the Prince of Peace.

Activity: Make an Advent Wreath

An Advent wreath is an integral part of Advent worship and consists of the wreath itself and four purple (or blue) candles, one for each Sunday in Advent. On Christmas Eve a white candle called the Christ candle is added, usually in the center of the wreath.

Today there are Advent wreaths available made of everything you can think of—metal, clay, straw, and so forth—and you have the option of purchasing your own to use year after year.

But there is nothing quite as symbolic as an Advent wreath made of live greenery, which itself represents eternal life. You might also want to use mistletoe, holly, or ivy to decorate your wreath because these evergreens bear fruit in winter. Holly is a symbol of Christ's Passion because its prickly leaves represent the crown of thorns.

You will need:

a foam circle	evergreens
floral scissors	florists' pins
a small knife	four candles (purple or blue, 8" or taller)
one large white candle and candleholder	

Purchase a ready-made foam circle to use as the base of your wreath. Use a small knife to cut four evenly spaced holes into the foam circle. (Be careful not to cut too deeply or too wide. Twist the candles into the holes to make sure they will fit, then remove the candles.)

Cover the foam circle with pieces of evergreen. Secure the pieces to the base with florists' pins (which can often be purchased at the same craft stores as the foam circles). Use your imagination and add any decorative touches you can think of.

Press the candles firmly into the holes in the wreath base. Light one candle for each Sunday of Advent. (On the first Sunday you will light one candle; on the second Sunday you will light two candles; and so forth.)

Set the Christ (white) candle on a candleholder or plate in the center of the finished wreath. Many people do not add this candle until Christmas Eve. Either way, do not light the Christ candle until Christmas Eve.

NOTE: Candles should never be left burning without an adult in attendance. Be sure to put all candles out immediately after each Advent worship service. Because of the fire hazard posed by live greenery, be sure to use artificial greenery if you meet in a public building.

Activity: Do-It-Yourself Litanies

A litany is a series of words of prayer or petition recited by a leader or a group, alternating with a fixed response by another group or the congregation.

Write your own litanies to use in your Advent worship. Here are a few ideas to get you started.

Choose a prayer response.
Write a litany of praise and use a well-known prayer response for the group response, such as, "We praise thy name, O Lord." Have at least four leader lines in your litany. For example,

Leader: We thank you for the special gift of hope that Jesus brings.
All: We praise thy name, O Lord.
Leader: We thank you for the special qualities of everyone in this group.
All: We praise thy name, O Lord.
Leader: We thank you for the joy of this special season.
All: We praise thy name, O Lord.
Leader: We thank you for our time together in your presence.
All: We praise thy name, O Lord.

Rotate leadoffs.
Instead of writing both parts of the litany yourself, post a well-known prayer response to use as the group response and ask several different people to each write a line or two. Then, when the group reads the litany, the people who wrote different parts would recite their lines and everyone else would repeat the response.

Leader #1: We thank you for all the gifts you bring us.
All: All praise to you, O God.
Leader #2: We thank you for health and happiness.
All: All praise to you, O God.
(And so forth.)

Divide a Bible verse.
Instead of having the group repeat a set response after each line of praise or petition the leader reads, choose an appropriate Bible verse and divide up the parts between the leader and the rest of the group.

Be creative! There are countless ways you can write your own litanies. Creating your own litanies will give your Advent worship times more personal meaning and help everyone feel more involved.

Activity: christmas Symbols Party

In order to better appreciate the many meanings of Christian symbols during this busy time of year, throw a Christmas symbols party. Fill your decorations and your activities with the Christian symbols of the season, and keep in mind that many different symbols—not just the Christmas ones—are appropriate for this time of year.

You will need:
    a Christmas tree of your choice
    craft supplies (such as felt, glue, polyfill, gold braid, red ribbon, paint, markers,
        sponges, and large rolls of white paper)
    party supplies and decorations (napkins, utensils, and so forth)
    refreshments
    adult volunteers

Christian Symbols Christmas Tree
Put up a tree (you can use anything from a traditional evergreen to a dead branch—anything you can come by easily that will meet your needs) and decorate it with Christian symbols. One of the easiest ways to make symbol ornaments for your tree is to photocopy the symbols from this book (you may want to reduce them in size) and cut them out to make patterns. Lay the symbol patterns on a double layer of felt, cut the shapes out of the felt, then glue or stitch the edges of the felt together, leaving an opening on one side so that you can stuff polyfill into the ornament. When the ornament is stuffed with polyfill, bend a piece of gold braid in half (to make a loop) and insert the ends into the opening on the ornament. Glue or stitch the opening together, and your ornament is ready to hang. Or, use the symbol patterns to make ornaments by any of your favorite methods.

Party Favors
Tie red ribbons around candy canes to give as party favors. Be sure to remind everyone that the candy cane is the symbol of the shepherds who visited the baby Jesus.

Symbol Napkins and Tablecloths
Make special napkins and tablecloths for your Christmas symbols party. To decorate white paper napkins with symbols, your group can draw symbols onto the napkins with magic markers, or you can sponge-paint symbols onto the napkins. Purchase pre-cut sponges from a craft supply store to use, or cut sponges into shapes yourself using reduced-size photocopies of the symbol patterns in this book. Lightly dip the sponges into tempera paint and touch them to the napkins. (It may help to dab the paint-soaked sponges onto paper towels first to soak up excess paint before touching them to the napkins.) Allow the napkins time to dry before using them for your party.

Use the same methods to make tablecloths for your Christmas symbols party. Use the rolls of white paper to cover the tables. Then tape the paper down and decorate it as you did the napkins.

A Galaxy of Stars
See page 14 of this book for this festive party-decoration idea.

Sing Christmas Carols
Put on your favorite Christmas music (or better yet, ask someone to play) and sing carols as a group. Point out how all Christmas carols are full of symbolism—stars, angels, shepherds, wise men, names for Jesus, the City of David, and so on.

Serve Symbol Cookies
Make a batch of your favorite cookie dough (or buy a roll of pre-mixed cookie dough at the store) and cut cookies into Christmas symbol shapes. Don't have symbol-shaped cookie cutters? Make copies of some of the symbols in this book, reduce them to the desired size, and cut out the symbol pattern. Place the pattern on top of the dough and cut around it with a knife. Remove the paper pattern and bake the cookies as you normally would.

Play Christmas Symbol Charades
See page 18 for a description of this entertaining party game.

Play Symbol Mix-up
Photocopy various Christmas symbols from this book (make two copies of each) and tape a symbol to everyone. (Make sure that there is a pair of people wearing each symbol.) Place your chairs in a circle, and ask everyone to sit on a chair. Choose the person whose birthday is closest to Christmas to be the Missing Symbol. Remove the Missing Symbol's chair from the circle. Then ask the Missing Symbol to start the game by calling out a symbol, such as "star" or "gifts." The two people wearing that symbol must get up and switch chairs while the Missing Symbol also tries to get one of the chairs. To stir up real confusion, let the Missing Symbol yell "Merry Christmas"—then everyone must get up and try for a new seat.

Give a Gift of Symbols
Give a gift of symbols and of yourselves. Make arrangements to take your group to a local nursing home or homeless shelter after your Christmas symbol party. Take the ornaments from the Christmas symbol tree to give as gifts to the people you visit. (If you visit a homeless shelter, you might want to take along a few more practical gifts as well.) When you arrive, sing some Christmas carols and share your symbol cookies with the people you visit.

Take Your Party on the Road
Instead of taking a trip *after* the Christmas symbol celebration, set up the entire party at a nursing home, preschool, or homeless shelter where everyone can enjoy the whole time together.

Note: Whenever you plan to transport other people's children you will need to be sure to obtain written permission from parents or guardians in advance.

Lent and Easter

Palm Branch

The palm branch has come to be the primary symbol associated with the celebration of Palm Sunday, when it is waved joyously in church processions to reenact Jesus' triumphal entry into Jerusalem and used to decorate the altar during worship. The palm branches used during Palm Sunday this year are burned down to ashes that will be used to mark crosses on the foreheads of believers during next year's Ash Wednesday service.

Activity: Burn Palm Branches

You will need:
    palm branches
    container suitable for burning palm branches
    matches
    container for ashes

This activity needs to be planned a year in advance.

Palm Sunday
After all the Palm Sunday services are finished, gather the palm branches and put them in a dry, safe place where they will be stored until the Sunday before Ash Wednesday.

The Sunday Before Ash Wednesday
The symbolically proper way to do this activity is to burn one palm branch at a time. Take each palm branch and crush or crumble it. Place the pieces in a container suitable to use for burning the branches—a long, metal charcoal starter with a handle, one that is usually set on a grill to start charcoal, works well.

Make sure that each leaf is completely burned to ash. Allow the ashes to cool. Then place the ashes in a container. Present the ashes to the pastor or the person in charge of the Ash Wednesday services. This year's Ash Wednesday service will be more meaningful for all who have participated in the preparation.

Palm Branch

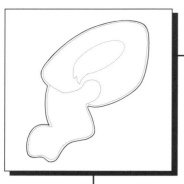

Basin and Towel

The basin and towel pattern reminds us of John 13:5, which tells the story of Jesus washing the feet of the disciples. The basin and towel represent Christ's love for us and his willingness to be a servant to all. This symbol is often used in the modern church to mean service to others.

Activity: Serving With Others

To actively experience what it means to serve others, plan and participate in a group service project. This project must include interaction with the people who are being served.

Take some time to research the church, community, and government organizations in your area to find what some of their greatest needs are, and choose one which calls for active participation.

Some possibilities to consider include:

Room in the Inn (or a soup kitchen): Prepare a meal for the homeless and the hungry. Do NOT stay in the kitchen after the meal is served, but get some food and spread out to eat and visit with the people you serve.

Local Community Center: Many local community centers are always in need of volunteers. Sometimes this volunteer experience can easily be a one-time event; other times they need their volunteers to be a dependable ongoing presence. Be ready to commit for a specified period of time.

Habitat for Humanity: Help build a Habitat for Humanity house (or, if the children in your group are too young to be allowed to work on the house, serve a meal to the volunteer builders). Be sure to meet the people for whom the house is being built and talk with them about their experience.

Your Church: Pick someone (or a group of people) in your church and help them clean their yard or repair their house; visit with someone who is ill or homebound; or take an older adult group to lunch.

Basin and Towel

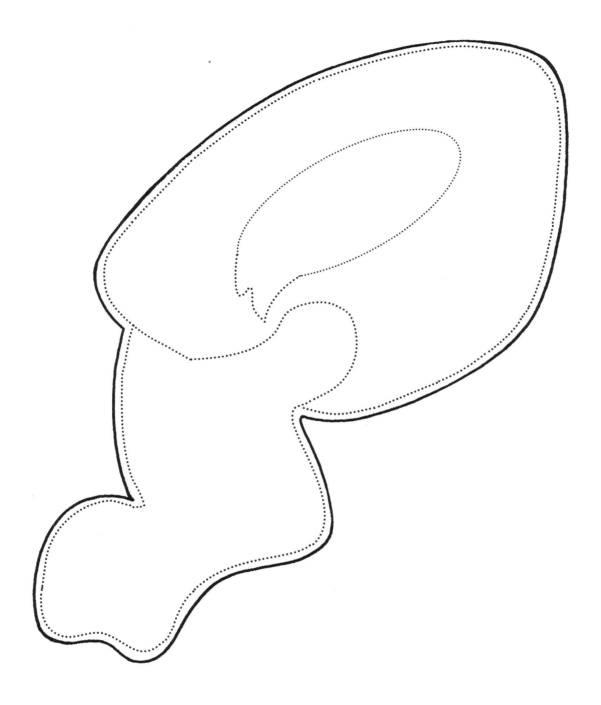

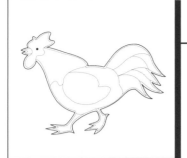

Rooster

The rooster (cock) reminds us of Peter's betrayal of Jesus (see Matthew 26:31-35, 69-75; Mark 14:27-31, 66-72; Luke 22:31-34, 54-62; and John 13:36-38). This betrayal of Jesus by the man upon whom Christianity was to be built was very upsetting, but Jesus knew that it would happen. The rooster symbol reminds us that it is always easier to say we will remain faithful than it is to actually remain faithful when the going gets tough. However, the rooster also reminds us that God knows this and that if we ask, we will be forgiven.

Activity: Banner Parade

There is something very awe-inspiring about hearing rousing Easter music and seeing beautiful flags paraded in and around the sanctuary or other gathering place. To help your group get more actively into the spirit of this meaningful time of year, organize a banner parade.

Ask every group in your church to choose one of the events of the Easter season and to design a banner that will be presented at the beginning (or end) of an upcoming Easter worship service.

Start this project at least three months in advance. You will need lots of advertising and cheerleading, as well as the help of a skilled organizer, to get everyone to participate. The banner parade project must also be coordinated with the pastor and the worship committee.

Photocopy symbol patterns from this book to use in designing the banners. Let each group choose how they want to design their banner; or, if they need help, assign each group one of the Easter (or church year) symbols to design their banner around.

Recommend to the groups that the banners be handsewn. Even children as young as kindergarten can handle making very large irregular stitches—and that just adds to the charm! If they do not wish to sew, then they could glue felt pieces onto a felt background, but the effect will not be as great. Have each group sew a backing onto their banner. This greatly enhances the banner's appearance.

Suggest that some groups use unusual fabrics such as wool, silk, and velvet on their banners. You will need to buy or make poles to hang the banners from as well as banner stands to set them in. Consider adding tassels to the banners or the poles.

Make plans to have representatives from each group carry their banners in a grand parade set to spirited Easter music on Palm Sunday or Easter Sunday. Have the group representatives circle around the sanctuary so that everyone can see the banners, then display the banners in their holders at the front of the church. The banners may be used in various ways in worship or classrooms for years to come.

Symbols of Faith

Rooter

Moneybag and Coins

Judas was considered the treasurer of the group of disciples (John 13:29), so a moneybag would be appropriate for his symbol. However, the purse (moneybag) and coins really represent the thirty pieces of silver Judas received for his betrayal of Jesus.

Activity: Decorating Crosses

Easter morning is a time for celebration. Decorate a cross to represent the Resurrection. Do it with joy and a little flare. You can choose one of the following crosses to decorate as a class, or you can divide your group into teams and assign each team a different "Symbol of Life" cross to decorate and have a parade of "Symbol of Life" crosses for Easter worship. Be sure to have stands ready at the front of the sanctuary where you can place the crosses after the parade.

FLOWERED CROSS
Cover a wooden cross with wire mesh. Have every participant or family of participants bring flowers from their garden. (Make sure to ask for ones with long stems.) Push the flowers stem-first through the wire mesh. (If you make this cross just for Easter morning, it won't need to last long, so don't worry about watering it. If you want to preserve it for a while longer you will need to put florist's foam behind the mesh.)

BELL CROSS
A fun way for children to celebrate Easter is to decorate a plain cross with colorful crepe paper or ribbon. Wrap the center pole in crepe paper or ribbon. Tie strips of crepe paper or ribbon in various colors to the arms of the cross and let them hang down in streamers. String bells onto yarn and tie them around the arms, letting them hang down like the streamers. This cross makes a wonderful, joyful sound when carried in a procession.

SYMBOL CROSS
Make reduced-size photocopies of any of the Easter symbols in this book. Color these symbols, decorate them, and attach them to the cross (whether you use tape, staples, glue, wire, and so forth will depend on the type of cross you use). Completely cover the cross with these symbols. (Another option would be to cut out construction-paper hearts, glue a symbol to each heart, and cover the cross with the hearts.)

BUTTERFLY CROSS
Make butterflies from tissue paper and chenille sticks and cover the cross with butterflies.

Note: It's possible to simplify these activities by making a cross from styrofoam and attaching the symbols with pins.

Moneybag and Coins

Crown of Thorns

The crown of thorns is a symbol of the humiliation Jesus suffered at the hands of the Roman soldiers when they put a crown of thorns on his head and mockingly "crowned" him "King of the Jews." This incident is described in the Bible in Matthew 27:29; Mark 15:17; and John 19:2, 5.

Activity: Stations of the Cross

The Stations of the Cross have been done with slight variations in various Christian denominations for centuries. Also called The Way, the Stations of the Cross commemorate the events of Jesus' arrest, trial, and crucifixion. Since the Stations of the Cross end with Jesus' death, this activity is usually undertaken on Good Friday (or even the Saturday before Easter).

For this activity, you will need to erect a cross and/or a visual symbol of the event described at each "stop." Along with the Scripture reading and meditation, you may wish to have music and prayer at each stop. Many denominational books of worship will include some type of Stations of the Cross. This activity may be done as an entire worship service, or as a separate Lenten activity. Ask your pastor for help in setting up this important experience. (Preteens especially are old enough to experience this worship activity in a very meaningful way.)

Stations of the Cross	Scripture	Summary
1) Jesus prays alone.	Luke 22:39-44	Take this cup from me.
2) Jesus is arrested.	Matthew 26:47-56	Have you come with swords?
3) Sanhedrin tries Jesus.	Mark 14:61-64	Are you the Christ?
4) Pilate tries Jesus.	John 18:33-37	Are you King of the Jews?
5) Pilate sentences Jesus.	Mark 15:6-15	Crucify him.
6) Jesus wears crown.	John 19:5	Here is the man.
7) Jesus carries his cross.	John 10:17-18	I lay it down of my own.
8) Simon carries cross.	Luke 23:26	Simon the Cyrene
9) Jesus speaks to the women.	Luke 23:27-31	Weep for yourselves.
10) Jesus is crucified.	Luke 23:33-34	Jesus on the cross
11) Criminals speak to Jesus.	Luke 23:39-43	Today you will be with me.
12) Jesus speaks to Mary, John.	John 19:25b-27	Woman, this is your son.
13) Jesus dies on the cross.	John 19:28-34	It is accomplished.
14) Jesus is laid in tomb.	John 19:38-42	There they laid Jesus.

Chart from *The United Methodist Book of Worship,* page 366.

Symbols of Faith

Crown of Thorns

Nails

As symbols, nails represent the nails that were used to crucify Jesus. Nails remind us of how real the suffering and death of Jesus was.

Activity: Pound Nails

You will need:
   large board
   large nails
   hammer

You will need to recruit an adult volunteer to be the "nail pounder" for this activity. This nail pounder should be someone very strong to better aid in evoking the imagery of the Crucifixion.

Have everyone sit very quietly with their eyes closed and contemplate Jesus' physical suffering. Read the passages about Jesus' crucifixion aloud from any one of the Gospels (Matthew 27:27-34; Mark 15:22-43; or Luke 23:33-46).

While you read the Crucifixion story aloud, have the nail pounder continuously pound nails into a board, slowly and methodically. (If you are able to use a wooden cross for this activity, the effect is even more powerful.)

Activity: Footwashing

You will need:
   basin
   pitcher of water
   towels

This activity can be done as people enter the room (much like the footwashing that took place in the Upper Room) or as a part of a worship service.

You will need a basin, a pitcher of lukewarm water, and towels. When the first person arrives, pour the water into the basin. (You may need someone available to help keep the water pitcher full.) Then ask that person to sit down and remove his or her shoes. Kneel and proceed to wash and dry the person's foot. That first person to have his or her foot washed is then asked to wash the foot of the next person, and so on so that each new arrival can experience both having his or her foot washed and washing another person's foot.

Note: To overcome any objections that wearers of pantyhose and tights may have to this activity, ask these people to remove only their shoes and then proceed to wipe their feet with a dry towel. (Another alternative is to wash their hands instead of their feet.)

Butterfly

The butterfly is a symbol of both the resurrection of Jesus Christ and eternal life. The butterfly leaves the cocoon in a new form, which symbolizes how we are transformed through Jesus Christ from death to new life.

Activity: Plant a Butterfly Garden

You will need:
> a location for a garden
> seeds
> water
> fertilizer
> willing workers

Do a little research and find out which flowers and plants you can plant in your area to attract butterflies. The Internet has many sites about gardening that are great sources for this type of information. You could also make a trip to your local library, or, better yet, talk to a good gardener.

Buy seeds for the plants and flowers you've discovered attract butterflies. Get your group together, prepare the soil, and plant and water the seeds. Be sure that arrangements are made for how and by whom the butterfly garden will be cared for. Divide up these gardening tasks and times if possible in order to give everyone a feeling of connection to this butterfly garden.

Not only will this butterfly garden be good for the environment, help increase and maintain the butterfly population, and provide beauty for all, but it will give your group the extra benefit of creating an ongoing, growing symbol of the new life God has promised us through Jesus Christ.

Butterfly

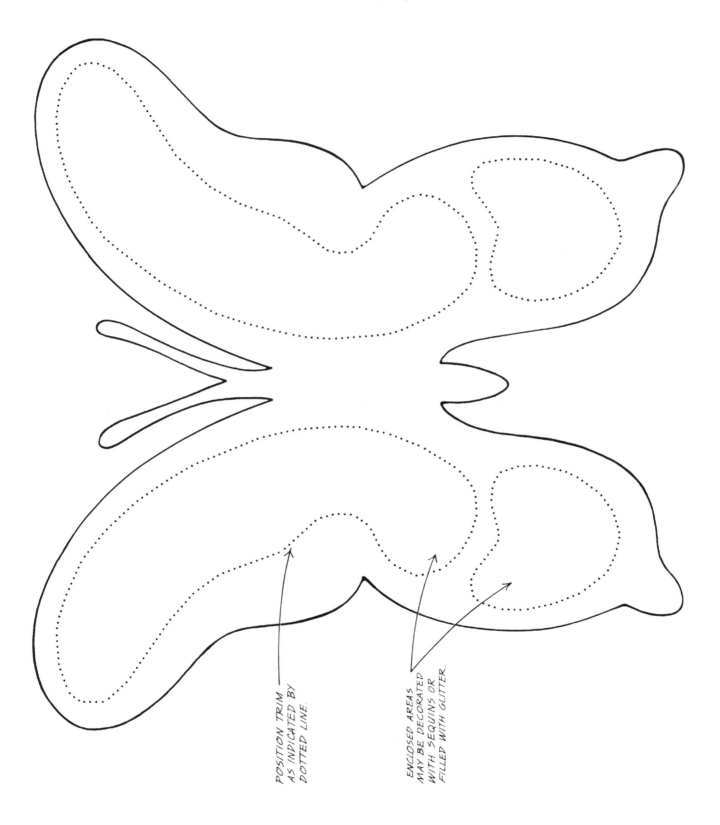

POSITION TRIM
AS INDICATED BY
DOTTED LINE.

ENCLOSED AREAS
MAY BE DECORATED
WITH SEQUINS OR
FILLED WITH GLITTER.

Symbols of Faith

Lily

The lily is a symbol of the Resurrection. The lily bulb decays in the ground over the winter, and yet from that decayed bulb new life appears in the spring. There are many colors of lilies, but the white lily is the one used as a Christian symbol. White stands for purity and joy. Most Christian churches decorate their altars or the fronts of their sanctuaries with white lilies for Easter morning services.

Peacock

The peacock has been a symbol of the Resurrection since the time of the early church. The peacock's beautiful feathers fall off (molt) and are replaced by new feathers that are brighter and more beautiful than the lost feathers. So it is with the Resurrection and new life. The new life provided through Jesus Christ is far greater than the life lost to us at our death.

Egg

Since the Middle Ages, the egg, often dyed and decorated for Easter, has been a symbol of the Resurrection. The egg holds new life within it. When the chick breaks through its shell, it breathes the air of new life. This breaking through the egg into new life has come to represent the resurrection of Jesus Christ.

Phoenix Rising

In legends about the phoenix, this bird dies in a great fire and then rises from the ashes to live again. In Christian symbolism the phoenix is shown with its wings spread in flight, rising out of the flames. Once thought dead, the phoenix lives again. Christians use the image of this legendary bird to point to the very real truth of Jesus' death and resurrection.

Activity: Holy Week Timeline

Use your wall space to make a timeline for Holy Week. This can be done as a simple timeline (with only days, event titles, and symbols) or as a timeline mural.

You will need:
Bibles
felt-tip markers
paints and paintbrushes (optional)

large sheets of paper
yardstick (optional)

TIMELINE

Divide the work among individuals or small groups. Let each group or individual choose one event from Holy Week, research where this event falls on the timeline, decide how to represent this event, and then add it to the timeline. If you are doing a simple timeline (listing only days and event titles), have each group or individual draw a symbol beside the listing of each event.

TIMELINE MURAL

If you are going to create a timeline mural, divide the work in the same way as for the simple timeline, but have the groups or individuals illustrate each event in detail in the appropriate place on the mural. (This activity could also be done as a permanent mural to decorate the wall of a hallway or classroom, but be sure to get permission from the church office first.)

Sunday

Jesus rides into Jerusalem on a donkey. *Matthew 21:1-11; Mark 11:1-11; Luke 19:28-40*
Jesus weeps over Jerusalem. *Luke 19:41-44*
Jesus returns to Bethany for the night.

Monday

Jesus curses the fig tree. *Matthew 21:18-22; Mark 11:12-14*
Jesus throws moneychangers out of the Temple. *Matthew 21:12-17; Mark 11:15-19; Luke 19:45-47*

Tuesday

Jesus teaches in the Temple courtyard and his authority is questioned by the Pharisees. *Matthew 21:23—22:46; Mark 11:27—12:37; Luke 20:1-44*
Mary anoints Jesus. *Matthew 26:6-13; John 12:1-8*

Wednesday (?)

Plot to betray Jesus. *Matthew 26:17-25; Mark 14:1-2, 10-11; Luke 22:3-6*

Thursday

The Last Supper of Jesus and the disciples. *Matthew 26:17-35; Mark 14:12-25; Luke 22:7-28; John 13*
Jesus prays in the garden of Gethsemane. *Matthew 26:30-46; Mark 14:26-42; Luke 22:39-46; John 19:1*

Friday

Jesus' arrest and trial by Sanhedrin, then Pilate. *Matthew 26:47—27:26; Mark 14:43—15:15; Luke 22:47—23:25; John 18:2—19:16*
Jesus is crucified. *Matthew 27:31-56; Mark 15:20-41; Luke 23:26-49; John 19:16-37*
Jesus is buried. *Matthew 27:57-66; Mark 15:42-47; Luke 23:50-56; John 19:38-42*

Sunday

Jesus is resurrected from the dead. *Matthew 28:1-15; Mark 16:1-8; Luke 24:1-12; John 20:1-29*

Pentecost

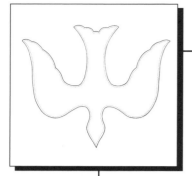

Descending Dove

The descending dove is the best-known symbol of the Holy Spirit. This symbol comes from the stories of Jesus' baptism. "And when Jesus had been baptized, just as he came up from the water, suddenly the heavens were opened to him and he saw the Spirit of God descending like a dove and alighting on him" (Matthew 3:16). All four Gospels report this event, which is proof of its significance.

The dove reminds us of Jesus' baptism. When we ourselves are baptized into the church, we ask that the Holy Spirit be active in our lives. The descending dove is also used on Pentecost banners as a sign of the Holy Spirit's coming at Pentecost. (See Acts 2:1-13.)

The dove symbol that we use to represent the Holy Spirit is always a descending dove (pointing down). This shows us that God comes to us.

Activity: Descending Dove T-shirt

You will need:
t-shirts   fabric puff paints
cardboard   pins
descending dove symbol pattern, page 45
or
t-shirts   crayons
computer with scanner and printer   iron-on transfer paper
iron   descending dove symbol pattern, page 45

Everyone will need to bring a new t-shirt that has been washed and ironed. Be sure to tell your group not to use fabric softener when washing or drying the t-shirts, because it makes it difficult for the paint or the transfer to adhere properly to the t-shirt material.

Puff-Paint Descending Dove T-shirt
Lay the washed and ironed t-shirt flat on the table. Place a piece of cardboard inside the t-shirt so that the paints do not bleed through. Place a copy of the descending dove symbol pattern in the center of the front of the t-shirt and secure it with pins to keep it from moving. Trace around the pattern with puff paints and allow it to dry. Want to have a small descending dove on the back shoulder of the t-shirt? Use a reduced-size photocopy of the pattern to trace a dove on the back of the shirt, once the front has completely dried. Don't forget to reinsert the cardboard inside the t-shirt before using paints.

Iron-on Descending Dove T-shirt
Ask someone to color the descending dove pattern, then scan the colored pattern into the computer. Fill the printer with iron-on transfer paper and print off one iron-on transfer for each member of your group.
Iron on the transfers by placing the colored side of the transfer on the t-shirt, ironing over the paper to press the image onto the shirt, then carefully peeling back the transfer paper. Images on transfers are reversed, but this will not matter with the dove symbol. However, if you wish to make a t-shirt with another pattern, remember to reverse the image on the computer before printing it onto the transfer paper.

Descending Dove

POSITION TRIM
AS INDICATED BY
DOTTED LINE.

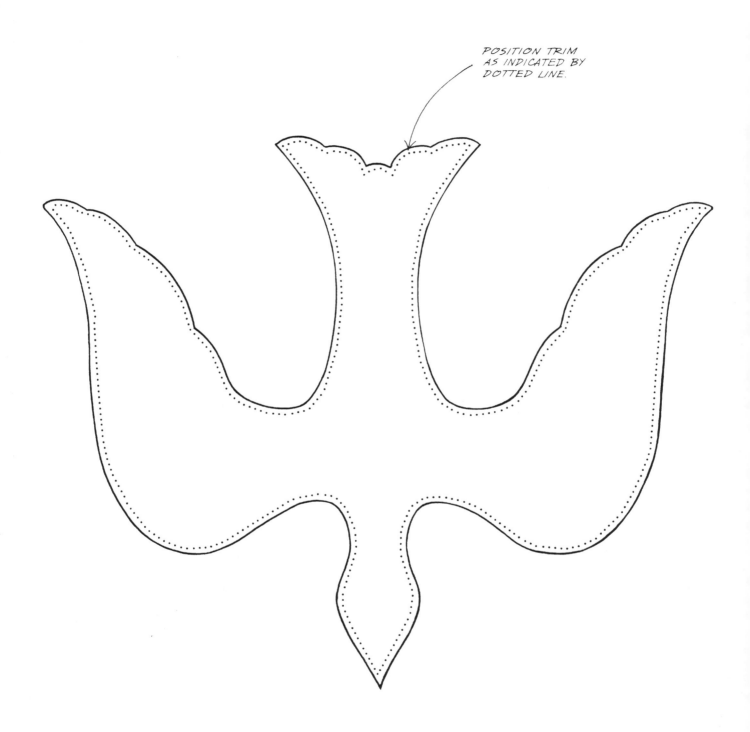

Flame

*The seven-tongued flame is another symbol of the Holy Spirit. Its meaning is based on the story of Pentecost in Acts 2:1-13. The seven tongues of the flame traditionally stand for the seven gifts of the Holy Spirit. These gifts have been associated with the gifts of the spirit referred to in Revelation 4 and 5 and named in Revelation 5:12—*power, wealth, wisdom, might, honor, glory, *and* blessing. *Another list of these gifts is found in Isaiah 11:2—*wisdom, understanding, counsel, might, knowledge, *and* fear of the Lord *(with* godliness *added to complete the list of seven gifts).*

Activity: Act out the Pentecost Story

You will need:
    Bibles
    items for making sound effects

Divide everyone into four small groups and give each group an assignment for the reenactment of Acts 2:1-15. (If you decide to act out the rest of Acts 2, you will need to have someone "preach" as Peter. If you do not want to do the entire sermon, skip to Acts 2:37-47 and finish there.) Choose someone who reads aloud well and expressively to act as the narrator. This person will read the entire story except for the parts that Peter and the crowd speak.

Group 1, disciples: Have this group scan the story (Acts 2) to find out what the disciples were doing, choose someone to play Peter, decide what the disciples were doing and when, and be prepared to act out their part of the story.

Group 2, crowd from all over the world: Ask this group to be prepared to play their parts. Let this group decide how to do this by scanning the text of Acts 2 to see what they would say and when. Be sure this group practices speaking in foreign languages (real or pretend) so that they can do so at the appropriate time.

Group 3, sound effects: Assign this group the task of producing sound effects at appropriate moments in the story. Have them check Acts 2 for places for sound effects such as wind (use a fan, or have everyone blow through their hands simultaneously) and fire (continuously crumble cellophane or something similar to achieve a crackling effect).

Group 4, props: Let this group look through the scripture passage and search the premises for things that Groups 1 and 2 could use as props. Let them use their imaginations and have a good time with their task.

This reading is fun to do either just for yourselves or for a larger audience. Have a good time with it. It's an important story that can come alive through the creative work of your group.

Flame

Puzzle Grid (Crossword / Word Search)

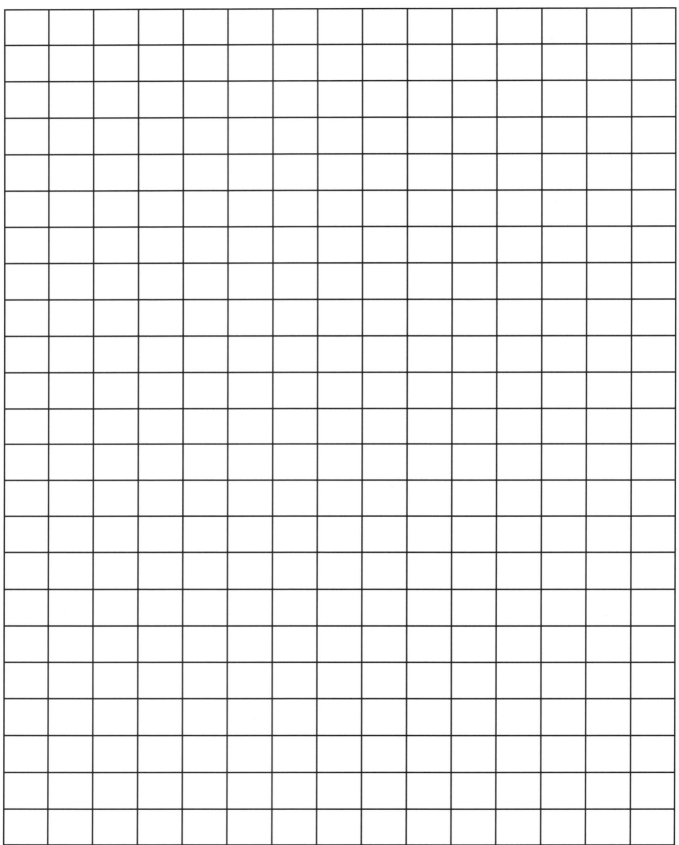

Symbols of Faith

Baptism

Water

Because it is essential to life, water has always been an important symbol. In Christianity, water is most often used as a symbol of baptism. We use water in baptism to "wash away" sin and allow the Holy Spirit to bring us to new life.

Activity: Water Centers

Set up several different stations in your room for a number of activities for learning about and experiencing water. As people enter the room have them visit these centers either individually or in small groups. After everyone has gotten a chance to experience all the water centers, bring the group back together for a discussion of water and its centrality to life. Close with worship.

Water Tasting
You will need:

photocopies of water-tasting form   several different types of water
plastic pitchers   cups
pencils

Make up a short water-tasting form to photocopy for each member of your group. This form should list the different types of water available to taste with a blank space after each where the person can write the number of the water they think corresponds to the type of water listed on the form. Have several different kinds of water in identical plastic pitchers (such as tap water, bottled water, soda water, water that has been boiled and cooled, seltzer water, well water, and so forth) set up on a table, and provide lots of small cups. Label each pitcher with a different number or letter (be sure to make a master list of which water goes with which number or letter). Ask each person to taste each water and mark on their sheet what kind of water they think it is.

Sounds of Water
You will need: CD/cassette player   CD/cassette of water sounds

You may purchase a CD or cassette of water sounds (often found in the meditation section) or you may make your own by recording the sounds of running tap water in a sink and in a bathtub, water dripping slowly from a faucet, splashing still water, a stream or waterfall, and so forth. Let everyone listen to the different water sounds.

Research
You will need: paper and pencils

Give everyone a sheet of paper and a pencil and ask them to list all the ways that water is used in your church. Have them explore the church to make sure they don't forget anything.

Water Experiments
You will need:

bucket of water   paper   oil, vinegar, food coloring, sugar, and so forth
spoons   bowls   towels
plastic tablecloth   pencils

At this center, participants will be pouring water into a bowl and then stirring one of the other available substances into the water. Then they should write answers to questions such as, Does the substance mix with water? How well does it mix? Which substance mixes with water most thoroughly and which separates from it?
Check your library (or a children's science book) for more fun and easy experiments like

this—the more unusual, the better. Be sure to post clear instructions for each experiment or have a helper at the center.

Water Relay Races

You will need: bucket of water   plastic drop cloth and masking tape (optional)
                   cups, glasses, spoons   towels or a mop
                   large empty container

Hold these races outside or cover the floor by taping down a large plastic drop cloth. Be sure to have plenty of clean-up equipment handy, such as towels or a mop.

1. Divide your group into teams and line them up single file at one end of the room. Place a large bucket of water and some small plastic or styrofoam cups in the center of the room. Set a large empty container for each team at the opposite end of the room. At your signal the first person on each team will run to the cups, pick one up and fill it with water from the bucket, run with the water to his or her team's container, pour the water in, then run back to the line and hand over the cup to the next person in line. The first runner then goes to the end of the line. If a cup tears or springs a leak, the runner must get a new cup and hand the new cup to the next runner. The first team to get their container full wins. (This can be tricky—a really fast team might lose because they spill more water.)

2. Divide the group into teams and have them line up single file at one end of the room. Place a container of water in front of each team and set one large glass for each team at the opposite end of the room. Give the first person in each team a spoon. At your signal the first runner for each team will fill the spoon with water, run to the team's glass, pour the water from the spoon into the glass, then return to the line, hand the spoon off to the next runner, and go to the end of the line. The first team to fill their glass wins.

Without Water

You will need: large sheet of paper and markers

Post a large sheet of paper on the wall of this center or lay the paper out on a table. Provide felt-tip markers and ask each person or small group to write down one thing they can think of that does not require water to grow it, make it, prepare it—or that just doesn't have any water in it anywhere. If they manage to put down anything at all, you will probably be able to come up with a way that it is associated with water after all.

Check the Bible

You will need:
   Bibles   concordance
   index cards   pens or pencils

Ask each person who visits this center to find one mention of the word *water* in the Bible and to write the Bible verse and reference on an index card. Ask everyone to bring their index cards with them to closing worship.

Worship

You will need:
   music source (such as hymnals)   index cards from "Check the Bible"
   clear tape

Close by bringing everyone back together for worship. Sing songs from your hymnal that you normally use for baptism. Ask everyone to read the Bible verses they found about water and then tape the index cards to the wall for display. (If there are too many people in your group to do this, choose a few participants to read their verses and ask everyone to post their index cards on the wall during the following hymn.) As a group, discuss what baptism means. Close with a hymn and a prayer.

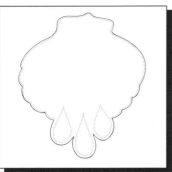

Shell

A shell with three drops of water (the three drops of water symbolize the Trinity) is a symbol for the baptism of Jesus.

Activity: Baptism Banners

You will need:
- photocopies of the shell symbol pattern
- felt
- paper
- scissors
- glue or needle and thread
- fabric paints or embroidery thread and hoops
- list of people baptized into your church in the current year, as well as the names of people about to be baptized
- small dowel rods with a hole in each end
- cord

Work together to decide how you will design your Baptism Banner (and if you will make one large banner or several personalized banners). You may choose to make one large banner that lists everyone who has been baptized into your church during the current year, or to make several smaller banners, one for each person who has been baptized. The shell is the most appropriate symbol for a Baptism Banner, but feel free to use another symbol or even to make a words-only banner.

Divide into groups either by task or by banner, depending upon the skill level of the members of your group. Let different groups work on one task for all the banners, or have each group complete one banner from start to finish.

Cut out a felt square for each banner, leaving approximately 1½" at the top of the square for folding over the dowel rod. Place the copy of the shell pattern (or, if you are putting words on your banner, letters that you have cut out of paper) on a second piece of felt and cut the symbol out of the felt. Arrange everything on the felt square to your satisfaction before gluing or sewing anything onto the banner.

Each banner should list the full baptismal names of the people who have been or will be baptized into your church during this current year, as well as the dates of the baptisms. You may want to paint or embroider these onto the banners. When your Baptism Banner is completed, fold the top edge of the felt square over the dowel rod and glue or sew it down. Run a cord (the length of the cord depends on the size of your banner) through the holes in the ends of the dowel, putting a knot at each end to hold the banner in place.

Ask your pastor for a time in worship when your group may present these personalized Baptism Banners as special remembrance gifts to the people baptized (or to their parents, if they are young children). If you made just one banner listing the names of everyone baptized, ask if you can present this to the entire congregation. Or, line a hallway or cover a bulletin board (depending upon the size of your banners) with the personalized Baptism Banners and leave them hanging for a full year.

Note: While the size, design, and materials of the banners will depend upon your group's abilities and available resources, the meaning of the Baptism Banners is the same for each one.

Shell

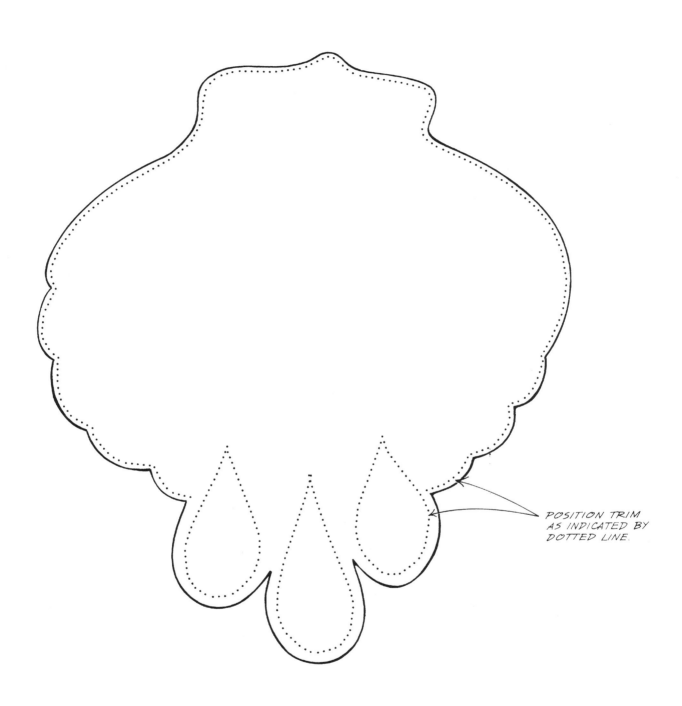

POSITION TRIM
AS INDICATED BY
DOTTED LINE.

Symbols of Faith

SYMBOL SEARCH FORM

THE SYMBOL	WHERE IT'S FOUND	ITS MEANING
_____	_____	_____
_____	_____	_____
_____	_____	_____
_____	_____	_____
_____	_____	_____
_____	_____	_____
_____	_____	_____
_____	_____	_____
_____	_____	_____
_____	_____	_____
_____	_____	_____
_____	_____	_____
_____	_____	_____

Symbols of Faith

Communion

Bread

Bread (more specifically, the bread used for communion) is a symbol for life. "While they were eating, he took a loaf of bread, and after blessing it he broke it, gave it to them, and said, 'Take; this is my body'" (Mark 14:22). This event is also reported in Matthew, Luke, and 1 Corinthians 11:23-26.

When a loaf of bread is shown accompanied by fish, we are reminded of the story of Jesus feeding the crowd with only a few loaves of bread and a couple of fish. This amazing meal can also be considered to be a type of communion.

This symbol also reminds us that Jesus called himself the Bread of Life (see John 6:35).

Activity: Bake Bread for Communion

You will need:
   your favorite bread recipe ingredients
   baking utensils
   a place to mix and bake bread

As a group make enough loaves of your favorite bread recipe to use for communion during Sunday morning worship (or at another worship time when communion is served). Be sure to get permission from your pastor and worship committee before you start this activity.

Let everyone contribute their abilities to bake the bread. Adults and children can work together to mix ingredients; kneading can be done in turns. However, all oven-related steps must be done by an older youth or an adult.

At the worship service you selected, process in as a group to present the bread for communion.

Use the recipe below if you'd like to try making your own unleavened bread (matzoh), a staple at Passover meals.

You will need:
   hot water
   flour
   salt
   plastic wrap
   electric skillet
   baking utensils and a place to mix and cook the matzoh

Mix together 1 cup of flour and a dash of salt. Stir ⅓ cup of very hot water into the flour mixture. Knead the dough quickly (don't overdo it). Cover the dough with plastic wrap and let it sit about five minutes while a skillet is heating to medium hot. Pinch off small balls of dough and flatten them with your hands. Cook the matzoh in the ungreased skillet until lightly browned, about two minutes on each side.

Symbols of Faith

Bread

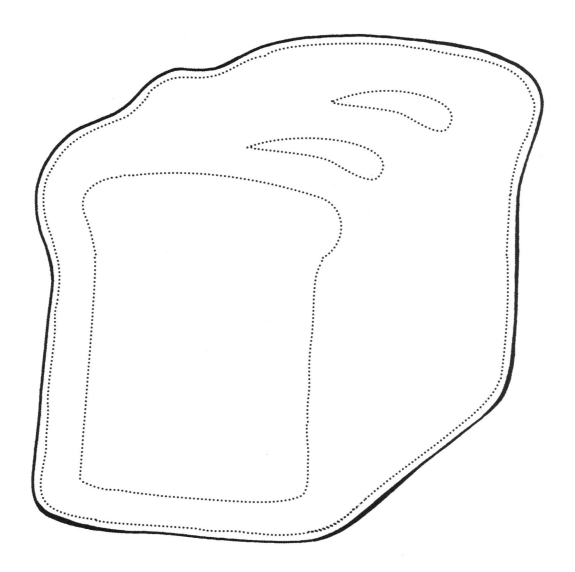

Symbols of Faith

Cup (Chalice)

According to Matthew, Mark, Luke, and 1 Corinthians 11:23-26, at the Last Supper Jesus took a cup and said, "This is my blood," and commanded his disciples to drink of it. The cup represents the Lord's Supper (communion) which is still served in every Christian church to this day, because Jesus told us that sharing the bread and wine is to be done in remembrance of him. Participating in communion reminds us of Jesus' sacrifice for us.

Activity: Communion Acrostic

You will need:
    large sheets of paper
    felt-tip markers

Use the word COMMUNION to create an acrostic. (Acrostics are made by writing a word vertically on a page and using each letter to write a one-line message or to explain more about the word.) This acrostic activity can be done either by working in one large group or by dividing into smaller groups to create several acrostics and then coming back together to share with everyone.

Help your group visualize this activity by writing the word COMMUNION vertically on a large sheet of paper and posting it where it can easily be seen. If you are splitting into small groups, ask everyone to copy the word just as they see it on their large sheets of paper. If you are going to make one acrostic for the entire group, then simply fill in the paper you have already prepared.

Here is a sample communion acrostic:

Coming together
Opening up to God
re**M**embering
co**M**fort from God
Uniting as one
se**N**ding Forth
serv**I**ce to others
H**O**ly Spirit
k**N**eeling in prayer

Cup

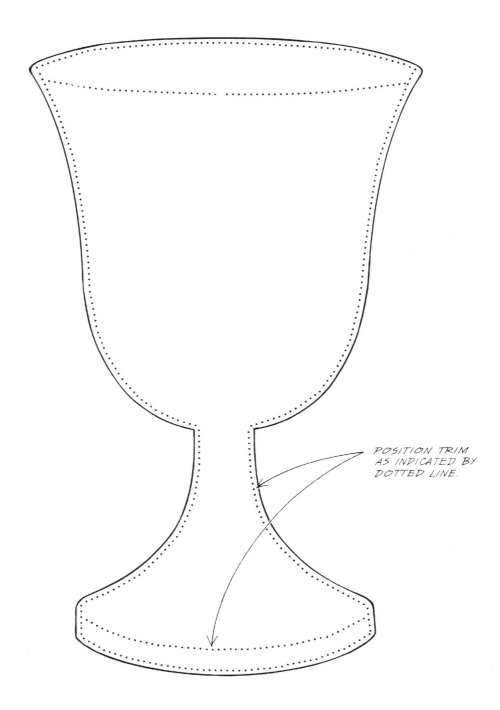

POSITION TRIM
AS INDICATED BY
DOTTED LINE.

Symbols of Faith

Wheat

Wheat symbolizes "plenty," having an abundance of what we need. In Christian symbolism a sheaf of wheat stands for Christ's body. In John 6:35 Jesus said, "I am the bread of life. Whoever comes to me will never be hungry." Wheat pictured with grapes stands for the bread of communion. See Matthew, Mark, or Luke for the story of the institution of the Lord's Supper, which we remember through our celebration of communion.

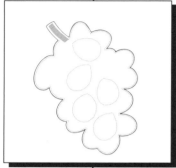

Grapes

A bunch of grapes symbolizes the communion wine. We usually see this symbol at the communion table. A sheaf of wheat and a bunch of grapes are often used together on banners and altar cloths to represent communion.

Activity: Appliqué an Altar Cloth

You will need:

the measurements of your church's altar
durable fabric in contrasting colors for
    altar cloth and appliqués
heavy, nonwoven, fusible interfacing
photocopies of patterns from this book
scissors
pencils
pins or tape
needles and thread
iron and ironing board
fabric glue (optional)
brown wrapping paper or
    construction paper (optional)

1. Choose the time of year when your altar cloth will be used. Research the colors of that season (see page 156) and decide on appropriate symbols. (If you plan on putting words on your altar cloth, you may want to make patterns for letters out of brown wrapping paper or construction paper.)

2. Use the main color of the season for the altar cloth itself. Choose colors that will stand out against the color of the altar cloth to use for the appliqués.

3. Adhere the fusible interfacing to the back of the appliqué fabric. Be sure to attach this to enough of the fabric that the back of the entire symbol or letter will be covered. This makes cutting and sewing the appliqués much easier, and makes the appliqués themselves lay better.

4. Place your pattern on the backside of the fabric (the side with interfacing) and trace the outline of your pattern on the interfacing. Cut out the symbol or letter—now you have your first appliqué!

5. Arrange the symbols and/or letters on the altar cloth. Tape or pin the appliqués in place. Drape the altar cloth over a table and step back to be sure everything is placed as you desire. Make adjustments as necessary. Then iron the entire altar cloth with the appliqués in place.

6. Sew the appliqués in place. (You may want to use a small amount of fabric glue to hold each appliqué in place while you sew.) Remove the pins or tape and iron the entire altar cloth one more time.

Wheat

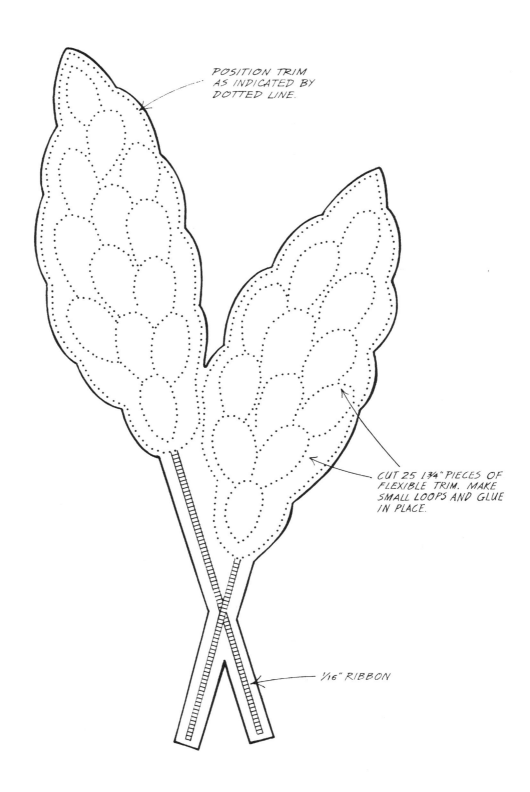

POSITION TRIM AS INDICATED BY DOTTED LINE.

CUT 25 1¾" PIECES OF FLEXIBLE TRIM. MAKE SMALL LOOPS AND GLUE IN PLACE.

¹⁄₁₆" RIBBON

Grapes

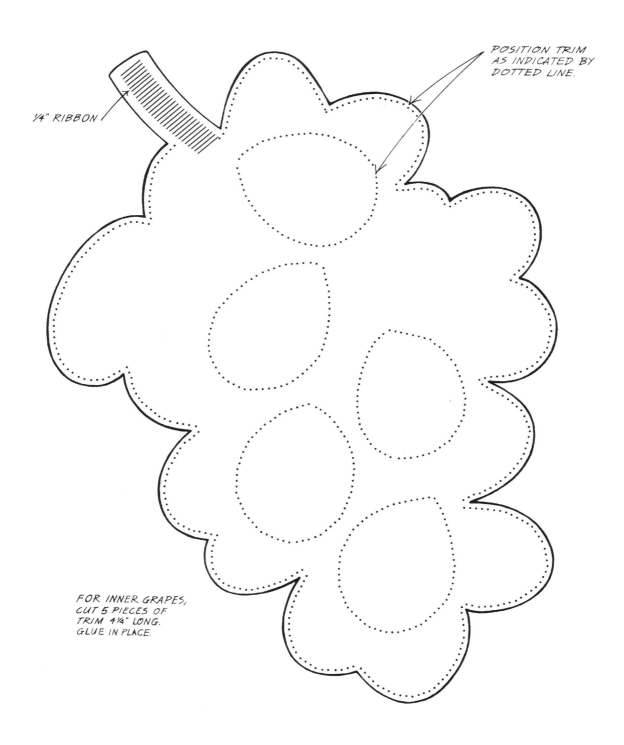

POSITION TRIM AS INDICATED BY DOTTED LINE.

¼" RIBBON

FOR INNER GRAPES, CUT 5 PIECES OF TRIM 4¼" LONG. GLUE IN PLACE.

Symbols of Faith

Crosses

Anchor Cross

After the Latin (Roman) Cross, the Anchor Cross is the oldest design for the Christian cross. Early Christians used the anchor—a sign of boats and the sea—like the fish symbol, as a secret message. The true meaning of these signs was hidden to all but other Christians. Where a non-Christian would see only an anchor, a Christian would also see the cross.

The Anchor Cross reminds Christians that Jesus died to bring new life. The Anchor Cross is a sign of hope in Jesus Christ. The hope symbolized by the Anchor Cross probably relates directly to Hebrews 6:19, "We have this hope, a sure and steadfast anchor of the soul."

Activity: Cross Treasure Hunt

You will need:
   pencils
   photocopies of the Symbol Search Form (page 54)
   pocket crosses

Make a game of discovering the many crosses in our midst.

Divide your group into teams. Give each team a copy of the Symbol Search Form (page 54). Set a time limit for their exploration (depending upon the size of your church).

Tell everyone that any kind of cross they find is acceptable, whether it's used in the sanctuary, in stained-glass windows, as art, as jewelry, or in signs.

When everyone has returned, go through their lists together. Give a point for each kind of cross they found, a point for each location where they spotted a cross, and a point for each meaning they came up with. Give everyone a pocket cross as a gift.

If you have transportation available, make this an event for an entire evening. Divide up into groups (with a responsible adult driver in each group) and have them scour the neighborhood as well as your own church. When everyone has returned, ask, "Did you see any uses of the cross that contradict the teachings of Jesus?" (This question is important because a symbol can be used by more than one kind of group and the symbol's meaning comes from the way it's used. Try to help your group understand that a symbol can sometimes be misused or misunderstood.)

Note: Use the Symbol Treasure Hunt to discover other symbols or types of symbols that can be found all around us!

Anchor Cross

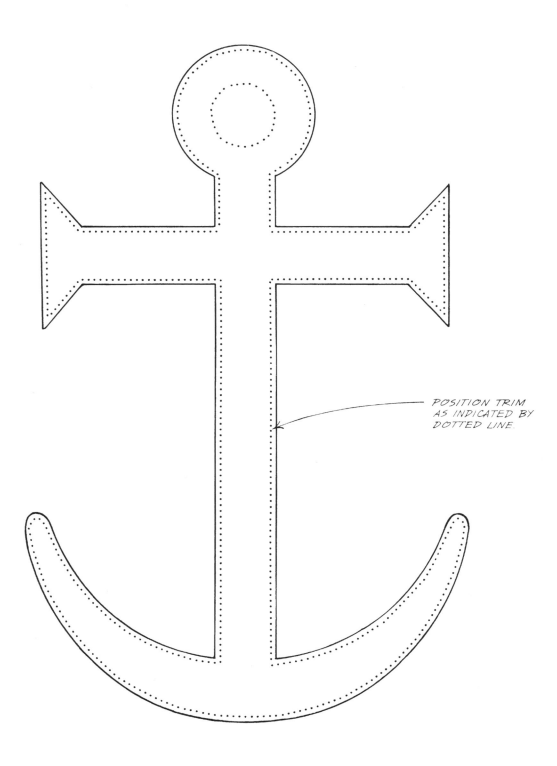

POSITION TRIM
AS INDICATED BY
DOTTED LINE.

Budded Cross

The Budded Cross is used as a symbol for either the young or the new Christian. When we see a bud on a tree or flower stem we know that a more mature leaf or plant will soon follow. The buds on the Budded Cross represent those young in the Christian faith who hold a promise of full "growth."

Activity: Symbol Bingo

You will need:
> photocopies of Symbol Bingo grid on page 92
> buttons, coins, or small scraps of paper to use as markers
> photocopies of all the symbols in this book (reduce these to fit the squares
>   on the Bingo Grid)
> container
> glue

You may want to make up the bingo cards ahead of time, or you can have the reduced-size photocopies of the symbols ready so that your group can make their own bingo cards.

Use photocopies of the Symbol Bingo grid (page 92) and reduced-size photocopies of all the symbols in this book to make bingo cards. Cut out the miniature symbols and glue a different symbol to each square on the bingo grid. It is not necessary to use categories for Symbol Bingo; but if you wish to, then be sure to assign each category a line on the grid before everyone starts gluing on the symbols. For example, instead of B I N G O, you might have CHRISTMAS, CROSS, EASTER, GENERAL CHRISTIAN, and OLD TESTAMENT. Make sure that everyone has put the symbols in the correct category.

Make a complete set of symbol cards for your bingo caller. The caller will need a symbol card for every possible symbol. Make these by photocopying all the symbols in this book and then writing the name of the symbol on each photocopy.

To play Symbol Bingo, the bingo caller will draw a card and call out the name of the symbol (if it's a cross, the caller will have to be sure to call out the specific type of cross). Play proceeds just like in regular bingo. The first player to cover an entire row is the winner. Be sure that everyone has enough coins, buttons, or scraps of paper to use as markers to cover the symbols.

REVERSE BINGO: Play Reverse Bingo as a fundraising activity. Ask everyone to bring lots of coins to use to cover the symbols on their cards. The winner of each round of Reverse Bingo must put all of the coins on his or her card into a large container. Donate all the coins that you collect to a mission. (You may want to have a good supply of coins on hand for making change.)

Budded Cross

POSITION TRIM
AS INDICATED BY
DOTTED LINE.

Symbols of Faith

Calvary Cross

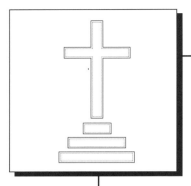

The Calvary Cross is formed by setting the Roman Cross atop three steps. This cross is sometimes called the Graded Cross. The three steps are often said to stand for faith, hope, and love.

Activity: Symbols Concentration Game

You will need:
- colored index cards
- photocopies of symbols (reduced-size)
- scissors
- pen
- glue

Make reduced-size photocopies of the symbols you want to review with your group. Cut colored index cards in half. (You can use plain white index cards, but colored ones are better because they are more difficult to see through.) Glue a symbol on one half of each index card, and write a brief summary of the symbol's meaning on the other half (keep the descriptions as short as possible, for example, "bread of life" for bread; "Holy Spirit" for the descending dove; "joy and celebration" for the palm branch; and so forth). Make sure you have a written description for each symbol. If you have a large group you may want to make more than one set of cards.

This game can be played by as few as two people or by a very large group (make at least one set of cards for every five or six players).

To play the Symbols Concentration Game, shuffle the cards and lay them out face down on a table. Proceed to play as you would any other memory matching game.

Are there any non-readers in your group? You could make a variation of this game especially for them by making a set of cards that have two of each symbol instead of a symbol card and a description card.

Another variation on this Symbols Concentration Game could help you teach your group the names of the symbols (such as the different types of crosses). Simply write the names of the symbols on the matching index cards instead of the descriptions.

Calvary Cross

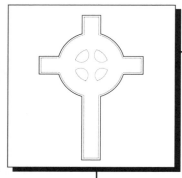

Celtic Cross

The Celtic Cross dates back to the early days of Christianity. Some of the best examples of the Celtic Cross are found in Ireland; in fact, this cross is often called the Irish Cross. The circle on the Celtic Cross represents eternal life. As Christians we believe in eternal life through Christ Jesus, and this cross is often used in cemeteries to show our belief that death is not the end.

Activity: A Collage of Saints Cross

You will need:
  an enlarged photocopy of one of the cross patterns
  instamatic camera and film
  posterboard
  glue
  paper and felt-tip marker

Photocopy and enlarge one of the cross patterns in this book. Send your group out to gather old photos of or to take pictures of the "saints" in your own church congregation, those who work for the glory of God in everyday ways. When the group returns, attach these pictures (cut to fit) to the enlarged cross pattern to make a collage. Mount the finished collage on posterboard along with a sign describing your group's definition of a "saint" and display the "A Collage of Saints Cross" in a prominent place in your church.

70

Celtic Cross

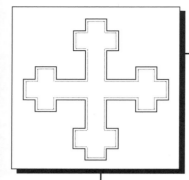

Cross Crosslet

The Cross Crosslet is basically four Latin crosses joined at their bases. This cross is used to represent the carrying of the gospel to the four corners of the earth.

Activity: Cross Quilt

You will need:
- different colors of solid-colored cloth or felt
- fabric scraps
- scissors
- needles
- thread
- photocopies of cross patterns
- dowel rod and cord (optional)

Make a true quilt.

If you know someone in your church who can quilt, ask him or her to help your group make a true quilt out of scraps of fabric. You might also want to ask each member of your group to bring pieces of fabric from old clothing.

Give everyone a square piece of solid-colored cloth to use as the background for their part of the quilt. Let each person choose one of the cross patterns you have photocopied and then cut the crosses from a different piece of fabric. Ask them to center each cross on their individual squares and then to sew the crosses to the squares (be sure everyone signs or embroiders their names on their squares). Then have the group sew all the squares together, adding a decorative border of contrasting cloth around the edges to finish off the quilt. (Remember that the sewing abilities of children and preteens are limited, so their stitches may be large and uneven—but this is part of the beauty of your community quilt.) You may even wish to send your quilt off to a service that can do the final quilting for you. Remember that making a quilt takes time!

Make a symbolic quilt.

Work with your group to make an attractive quilt-like hanging. Unlike a true quilt, this will be much simpler and give only a "quilt" impression. Give each person two squares of felt (in two different colors) and a cross pattern. Have them cut the cross out of one square of felt and sew it onto the other square. Have all the group members sign or embroider their names on their squares. When everyone is finished, work together to sew the squares into a quilt. Complete your symbolic quilt by sewing a strip of cloth around all the edges. You may even want to hang this symbolic quilt from a dowel rod for display.

Cross Crosslet

Jerusalem Cross

The Jerusalem Cross is formed by one large cross with four small crosses between the arms. This cross was on the coat of arms of the crusaders who ruled Jerusalem from 1099–1203 A.D. Some say that the large center cross represents the wound from the sword that penetrated Jesus' side and the four small crosses represent the wounds from the nails in Jesus' hands and feet. Others say the four small crosses represent the four Gospels.

Activity: Make a "Stained-Glass" Cross

You will need:
- photocopies of the cross patterns
- crayons
- black felt-tip markers
- vegetable oil
- cotton balls
- old newspapers
- rulers
- construction paper or posterboard
- scissors

Let everyone choose a cross pattern they like. Ask them to outline their cross with a black felt-tip marker and to also use the black marker to define sections of the cross in stained-glass style. Have everyone use crayons to color their "stained-glass" crosses. The harder they press on the crayons, the better "stained glass" it will make. In order to make the "leaded" lines stand out, have everyone trace over the black marker outlines with a black crayon.

Spread old newspapers on top of your table. When everyone has finished coloring their crosses, have them lay the crosses on top of the newspapers, drench a cotton ball in vegetable oil, and rub it completely over the colored side of the crosses. Make sure that the entire cross is thoroughly covered. Place the crosses on a fresh layer of newspaper to dry. You may have to wait until your next meeting to finish this activity.

When the crosses are dry, have everyone make a frame for their stained-glass creations. An easy way to make a frame is to measure the art and then cut construction paper (or posterboard) into four strips to fit around the edges. Then have them glue the strips along the edges of their stained-glass creation. Hang the crosses in a window that gets a good bit of light—the "stained glass" will shine and glisten in the sunshine.

Jerusalem Cross

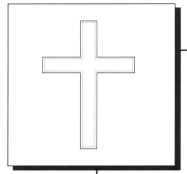

Roman Cross

The Roman Cross is the most commonly used form of the cross and the most recognized symbol of Christianity. While the cross is the symbol of Jesus' death and suffering, the empty cross also represents the Resurrection, the triumph over death.

Activity: Hot Cross Buns

An ancient tradition for the Lenten season is making and eating hot cross buns. These buns got their name because the icing was applied to the hot pastries in the form of a cross.

Have a Feast
Get together as a group to make hot cross buns. (Since the dough must sit in the refrigerator overnight before baking, you may want to make the dough yourself and just bake and ice the buns as a group.) Serve the fresh buns as refreshments for a Lenten study. This could be the beginning of a new tradition at your church.

Have a Sale
Take orders ahead of time for hot cross buns (to be delivered on Good Friday or the Saturday before Easter) for an Easter morning treat. Sell them by the dozen or half dozen. Be sure to have plenty of large resealable plastic bags available to put the buns in. The money earned from this project can go to help with any mission or service project that you agree upon beforehand.

Hot Cross Buns

½ cup milk
2 Tbs water
½ cup butter
2 packages of dry yeast
½ cup sugar
1 tsp. salt
1 tsp. cinnamon

½ tsp. nutmeg
3¼ cups flour (unbleached)
4 eggs
1 cup raisins
vanilla frosting (see recipe
  below)

Heat milk, water, and butter in a saucepan to 105–115°F. Put the yeast in large bowl; add the milk mixture to the yeast. Stir in the sugar, salt, cinnamon, nutmeg, and 1 cup of flour. Beat at medium speed for 2 minutes. Add ½ cup flour, 3 eggs, and 1 egg yolk (save the egg white). Beat at medium speed for 2 minutes. Stir in the remaining flour and the raisins. Dough will be soft. Put the dough in a clean, greased bowl, cover, and refrigerate overnight. The next day with floured hands shape the dough into 2" balls. Place these on a greased baking sheet, brush the tops with egg white, and let rise until light. Bake at 350°F until golden brown (approximately 15 minutes). While the buns are warm, drizzle frosting in the form of a cross on the tops. Cool.

Vanilla Frosting
Mix together 1 cup powdered sugar, ¼ teaspoon vanilla, and enough milk to make a fairly stiff frosting.

Symbols of Faith

Roman Cross

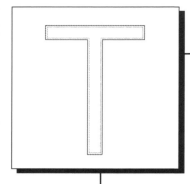

Tau Cross

The Tau Cross is the original form of the cross as a symbol. The Tau Cross gets its name from its resemblance to the Greek name for the letter T. *The Tau Cross is sometimes called the Old Testament Cross. The Bible tells us that Moses ordered the Israelites to make a sign on their doorposts with lamb's blood so that the firstborn of Israel would be spared when the firstborn of the Egyptians were killed. According to tradition, this sign was a cross that looked like the letter* T.

It is also believed that the pole on which Moses set the bronze serpent (Numbers 21:8-9) was a Tau Cross. The Tau (or Old Testament) Cross gives us a strong link between Jewish and Christian traditions.

Activity: Research the Word Cross

You will need:
- Bibles
- pencils
- paper
- tape
- concordance (optional)

Give each member of your group a sheet of paper and a pencil. Ask everyone to look up the word *cross* in the concordance, choose a passage, and write down the book, chapter, and verse that they have chosen. As each person chooses a passage, have him or her sign his or her name to the paper and tape it to the wall so that everyone can see what's already been chosen and pick a different verse. When everyone has found a passage, have them each look up their verses in the Bible. When everyone has located their verse, ask them to each read aloud the passage they chose.

If you don't have a concordance handy, assign one of the following Bible verses to each person in your group.

Matthew 10:38	John 19:17-20
Matthew 16:24	John 19:25
Matthew 27:32	John 19:31
Matthew 27:40-42	1 Corinthians 1:17-18
Mark 8:34	Galatians 5:11
Mark 15:21	Galatians 6:14
Mark 15:30	Ephesians 2:16
Mark 15:32	Hebrews 12:2
Luke 9:23	1 Peter 2:24
Luke 14:27	
Luke 23:26	

Tau Cross

Symbols of Faith

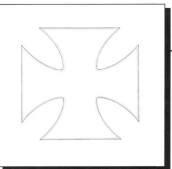

Cross Pattée

This very beautiful form of the cross is often used for decorative purposes whenever the decorative use of the cross is appropriate.

Cross and Crown

This cross and crown (note that the crown is placed in front of the cross) together symbolize the reward to the faithful, those who believe in the crucified Savior, in life after death. "Be faithful until death, and I will give you the crown of life" (Revelation 2:10).

Activity: "Wired" Cross

You will need:
- small craft sticks in two lengths
- paints and paintbrushes
- copper wire
- wire cutters
- glue
- small magnets (optional)
- glass or plastic beads (optional)

Give everyone two craft sticks, one of each length, and have them paint each craft stick a bright color. When the paint is dry, show them how to use the shorter craft stick as the crossbar for the cross and the longer one for the upright beam of the cross. Have everyone put a dab of glue on one of the craft sticks and glue the crossbar to the back of the longer craft stick. Let the crosses dry for a couple of minutes.

Wrap each cross with two pieces of copper wire. You will need one piece to wrap the crossbar and a longer piece to wrap the upright beam. On the back of the cross wrap the wire up one side of the bar or beam and then down the other. This will secure the crossbeam to the upright pole of the cross.

You may want to buy small magnets (available at any craft store) for your group to glue onto the back of their "wired" crosses so that they may more easily display them at home. If you'd like to try a colorful variation on this project, thread glass or plastic beads onto the wire before wrapping it around the cross.

Cross Pattée

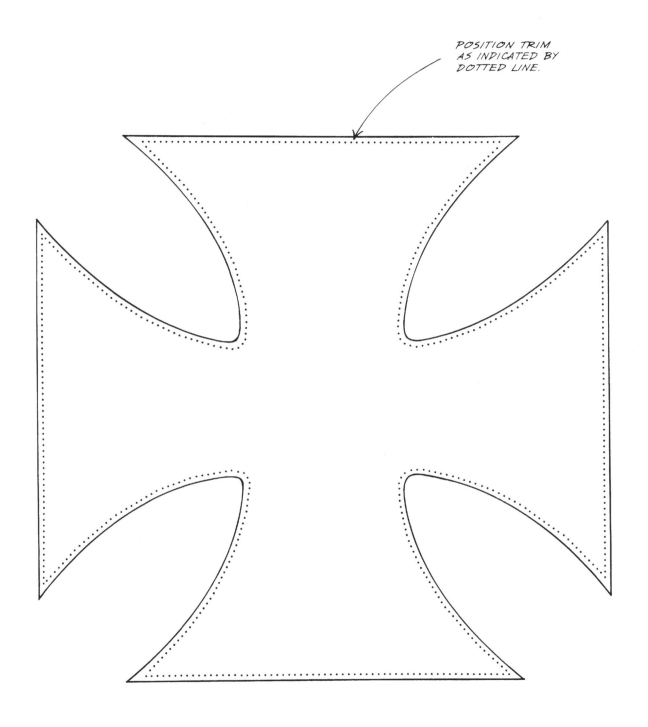

POSITION TRIM AS INDICATED BY DOTTED LINE.

Cross and Crown

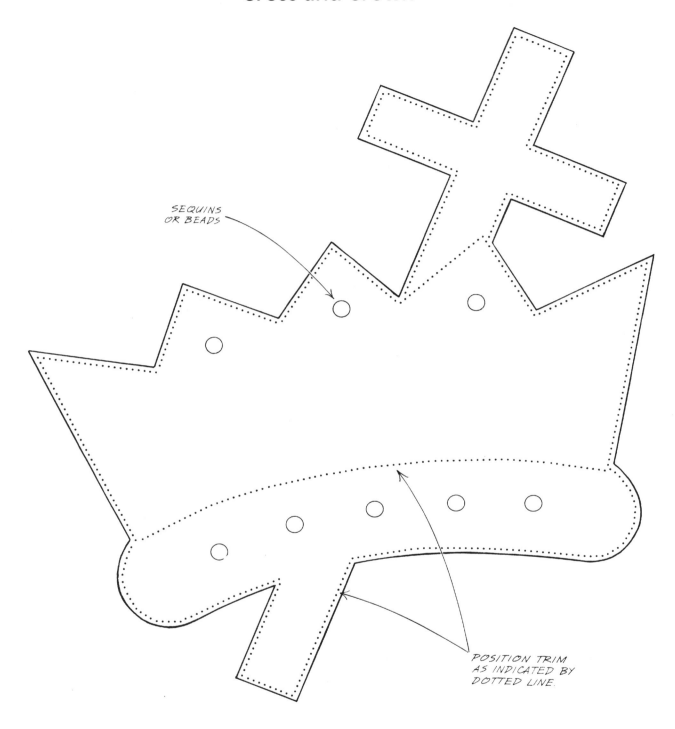

SEQUINS OR BEADS

POSITION TRIM AS INDICATED BY DOTTED LINE.

Symbols of Faith

Symbols
for
Jesus

Alpha and Omega

These two letters (which look like an A and an upside down U and here are put together into one) are the first and last letters in the Greek alphabet—the Alpha and the Omega (A and Ω). These two letters are used by Christians as a sign of God's omnipotence (all-powerfulness), "'I am the Alpha and the Omega,' says the Lord God, who is and who was and who is to come, the Almighty" (Revelation 1:8). When the Alpha and Omega symbol is used with another symbol for Christ (the cross, the Chi Rho, and so forth), it specifically represents Christ. "I am the Alpha and the Omega, the first and the last, the beginning and the end" (Revelation 22:13).

Activity: The Alpha and omega Hour

Arrival Activity
List (or cut pictures from magazines) several activities (for example, a series of "getting ready for work" activities would include getting out of bed, taking a shower, brushing teeth, eating breakfast, getting dressed, and so forth) on a series of index cards and have the group attempt to put the activities in proper order from first to last.

Game
- Play any type of relay game where the object must be passed from the first to the last person and then finally brought to the front of the room. Let everyone have the chance to be both first and last.

- Play a game of Reverse Follow the Leader. Have everyone line up single file. Start the game as usual with the first person in line acting as the leader. However, when you yell, "Reverse!" the last person in line becomes the leader—only tell the group that they can't turn around to see what that person is doing, so they have to get their clues verbally, by looking over their shoulders, and so forth.

Craft
Make a simple alphabet book (with a letter of the alphabet on each page, along with a few pictures of items starting with that letter) to give to the church nursery or to a needy mother with a baby.

Bible Verse Memorization
Line out either of the Bible verses printed above. "Lining out" a verse is a memorization activity that is often used with nonreaders. The leader starts by saying part of the verse, which is then repeated by the group. Gradually the leader adds each additional part of the verse with everyone repeating until finally the leader is saying the entire verse and the group can repeat the entire verse back. For example, with Revelation 1:8, the leader would start by saying "I am" (the group repeats); then "I am the Alpha" (the group repeats); and so on.

Discussion
Have everyone form a straight line. Designate the person at one end of the line as "first" and the person at the other end of the line as "last." Have "first" and "last" walk toward each other so that they lead everyone together to form a circle. After the circle comes together, ask, "Does it matter at this point who is 'first' and who is 'last'?" Ask everyone to sit down (still in a circle) and ask, "Why do we think it is so important to be first in everything? Why is it important that Jesus is the first and the last, the beginning and the end?"

Symbols of Faith

Alpha and Omega

POSITION TRIM
AS INDICATED BY
DOTTED LINE.

Symbols of Faith

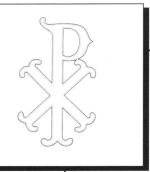

Chi Rho

The Chi Rho (pronounced ky-row) is the oldest monogram for Jesus Christ. This monogram is formed by placing the Greek letters Χ (chi) and Ρ (rho) together. The Χ and Ρ are the first two letters of the Greek word for "Christ." The full Greek word for Christ looks like this: ΧΡΙΣΤΟΣ. Constantine, the first Christian emperor of Rome, had the Chi Rho placed on the banners of the Roman infantry.

Activity: Symbols of Jesus Door

You will need:
- large roll of heavy brown paper or heavy decorative wrapping paper
- tape
- scissors
- construction paper, posterboard, or felt
- art supplies
- photocopies of the symbols for Jesus patterns
- glue

Cover your door with a display of the names and symbols for Jesus, which will serve as testimony to all who pass by of the love that Jesus brings.

Divide your group into teams and assign each team one or more tasks.

1. Completely wrap the outside of the door, either with plain brown paper (let your group make it more decorative as work progresses) or in gift-wrapping paper (to look like a gift).

2. Use the photocopied symbol patterns to cut symbols for Jesus from construction paper, wrapping paper, felt, or whatever other material you choose.

3. (This task is optional.) Decorate the symbols by coloring them with crayons or markers, trimming them with gold braid, making them shine with glitter glue or metallic paints, and so forth.

4. Attach the finished symbols to the door. The group who does this task will also need to decide if anything will be written on the door. If they want to include a message or some of the names for Jesus, then they should either write directly on the paper the door is wrapped in, write on a piece of posterboard, or cut letters out of construction paper.

Symbols of Faith

Chi Rho

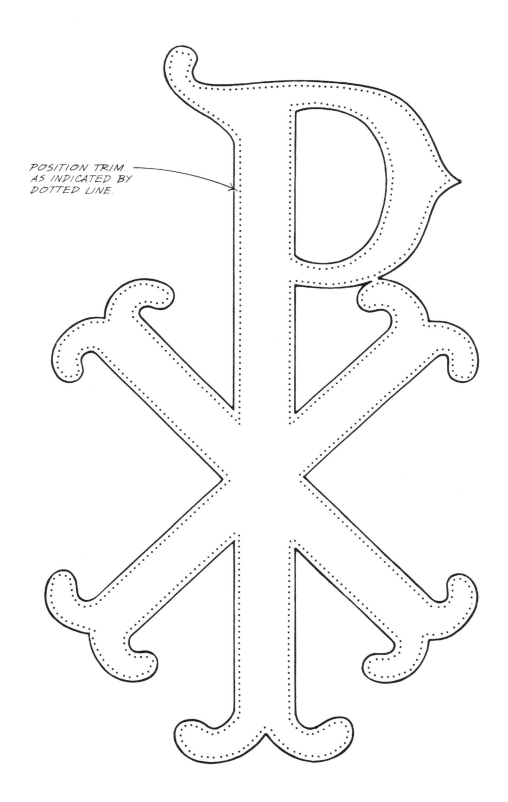

POSITION TRIM AS INDICATED BY DOTTED LINE.

Jesus Monogram

The Jesus monogram is an acrostic formed by each of the five Greek words for Jesus Christ, Son of God, Savior.

I for the Greek word for *Jesus.*
CH for the Greek word for *Christ.*
TH for the Greek word for *God.*
U for the Greek word for *Son.*
S for the Greek word for *Savior.*

alpha= $\mathrm{A}\alpha$　　iota= $\mathrm{I}\iota$　　rho= $\mathrm{P}\rho$

beta= $\mathrm{B}\beta$　　kappa= $\mathrm{K}\kappa$　　sigma= $\Sigma\sigma$

gamma= $\Gamma\gamma$　　lambda= $\Lambda\lambda$　　tau= $\mathrm{T}\tau$

delta= $\Delta\delta$　　mu= $\mathrm{M}\mu$　　upsilon= $\Upsilon\upsilon$

epsilon= $\mathrm{E}\epsilon$　　nu= $\mathrm{N}\nu$　　phi= $\Phi\phi$

zeta= $\mathrm{Z}\zeta$　　xi= $\Xi\xi$　　chi= $\mathrm{X}\chi$

eta= $\mathrm{H}\eta$　　omicron= $\mathrm{O}o$　　psi= $\Psi\psi$

theta= $\Theta\theta$　　pi= $\Pi\pi$　　omega= $\Omega\omega$

Symbols of Faith

Jesus Monogram

I.N.R.I.

INRI is a monogram for Jesus that started at the Crucifixion. When Jesus was crucified, Pilate ordered that an inscription be placed on the cross above Jesus' head. The inscription was done in three languages—Greek, Latin, and Hebrew. The letters INRI *stand for the Latin words* Iesu Nazrenus Rex Iudaeorum. *This translates into English as "Jesus of Nazareth, King of the Jews."*

Activity: Jesus in Song

You will need:
  hymnals
  songbooks
  piano or other instrument (optional)

Divide your group into small teams and have them search the hymnals and songbooks for songs that use different names for Jesus. See which team can find the most names. Be sure that they actually read the entire text of the songs and the hymns they come across as they may find additional names in the body of the songs or hymns.

Some possibilities for songs and hymns include:
    O Come, O Come Emmanuel
    Savior, Like a Shepherd Lead Us
    Precious Lord, Take My Hand
    Jesus, Name Above All Names
    Christ the Lord Is Risen Today
    Majesty, Worship His Majesty
    All Hail King Jesus

Be aware that you will probably not find all of these songs in one single book.

Symbols of Faith

Activity: Who Is Jesus? Poster

You will need:
  Bibles
  posterboard
  felt-tip markers
  index cards
  pen

You may have your entire group work as a whole to make a large poster for the worship area, or you can divide into groups to make smaller posters for the walls of your meeting area.

Before you meet, write Bible references for several of the names for Jesus on index cards.

1. Have the group write in the middle of the poster, "Who Is Jesus?"

2. Divide the index cards up among the group members and ask them to look up the Bible passage listed and write the name or title for Jesus that they find on the poster. Ask them to note each Bible reference beside or underneath the name for Jesus in that passage. Or, if you are making several smaller posters, either assign one Bible reference per poster or put the index cards in a pile and let the groups draw one for each poster. Then they should look up the Bible reference and write the name for Jesus and the book, chapter, and verse on their poster.

3. Have everyone work to decorate the poster. When they are finished, display it in a prominent location.

Some possible Bible references to use include:
  Matthew 12:8—lord of the sabbath
  Matthew 20:31—Son of David
  Luke 19:10 and John 1:51—Son of Man
  John 21:7, Matthew 8:25, Acts 16:15—Lord
  John 1:1—the Word
  John 6:48—bread of life
  John 8:12—light of the world
  Acts 2:36—Lord and Messiah
  Revelation 22:13—Alpha and Omega
  Revelation 22:16—the bright morning star
  Revelation 22:16—the root and the descendant of David

Symbol Bingo

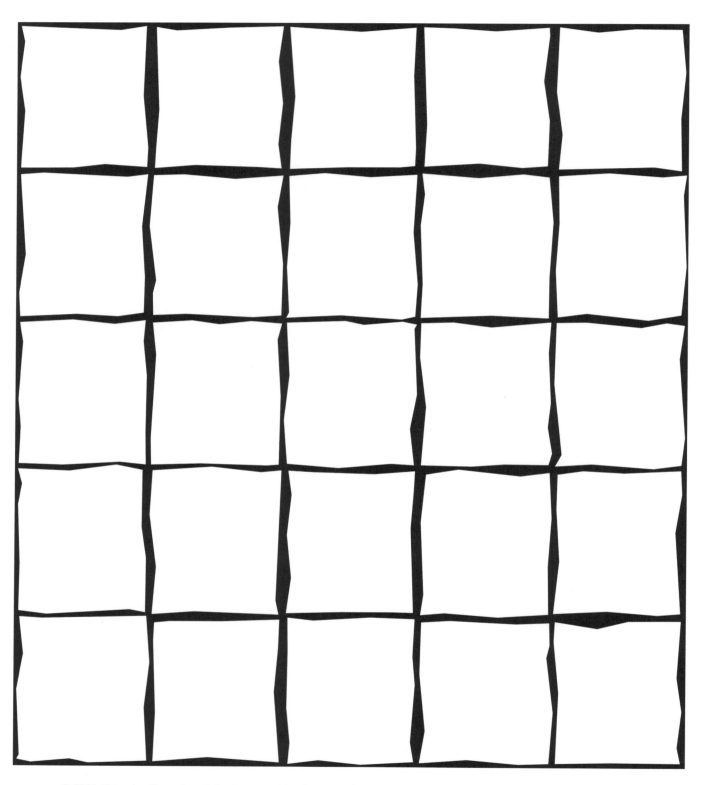

Symbols of Faith

The Trinity

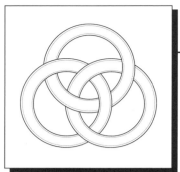

Entwined Circles

Three entwined circles are a symbol of the Trinity. The overlapping three circles represent the three natures of God—Father, Son, and Holy Spirit. The circle itself stands for the eternal nature of God. The circle has no beginning and no end, just like God.

Activity: Play With circles

You will need:
  hula hoops
  paper cups and/or plates
  paper
  crayons or markers
  game equipment

Hula Hoop Relay Race

Get some old fashioned hula hoops (yes, you can still find hula hoops at toy stores and discount stores), divide into groups, and give each group a hula hoop for a hula hoop relay race. Tell the racers that they can only move forward while keeping the hula hoop up by swaying their hips. (If they drop the hula hoop, though, let them pick it up and continue from that point rather than having to start over—some of us just aren't coordinated enough to to do this well.)

Circle Art

Give everyone a piece of paper, a crayon or marker, and a paper plate or cup. They will be using the paper plates or cups to help them draw perfect circles. Have everyone draw a circle on the paper by tracing around the plate or cup. Then turn them loose. Tell them to them use their imaginations to make a picture out of the circle (the circle could become the sun in a landscape, or a car headlight, or a person's face, and so on). (Or, for a variation on this art activity, have everyone draw a picture that is entirely composed of circles. This can be quite challenging!) Display the circle pictures in your own group "art gallery." Be sure to "ooh" and "aah" over every piece of art (even if all someone could think of to do with the circle was to make a smiley face).

Circle Games

Play any circle game that you have equipment and space for. A circle game is one that's played in a circle, such as musical chairs, electricity, any sort of passing objects around a circle or keeping balls in the air, and so forth.

Entwined Circles

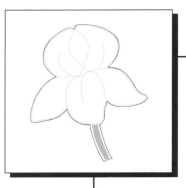

Iris

This flower is often used as a symbol for Mary, the mother of Jesus, because it represents purity.

The iris is also often used as a symbol for the Trinity. The iris usually has three upright standards (petals) and three petals that drape downward. In non-stylized art of the iris, the third standard at the top appears at the back side of the iris. Each set of three represents the Trinity.

This symbol for the Trinity may have come into widespread use because it was the emblem of the French royal family. Their use of the iris led to its numerous appearances in religious art.

Activity: Plant an Iris Garden

You will need:
    iris bulbs
    a well-prepared plot of ground
    fertilizer
    water
    a commitment to weeding!

Find a place for your group to plant an iris garden. If you wish to plant your garden on church grounds, be sure to get permission from the church office first, as well as an assigned location. Also, secure a commitment from your group members to take turns caring for the iris bed. (A variation on the iris garden activity could be to plant one symbolic iris in an existing flowerbed—with permission, of course.)

Perhaps your group would like to do this symbol activity as an ongoing service project for an elderly member of your congregation or for someone with limited mobility. The sight of a few irises blooming each spring is a wonderful reminder of renewed hope, of the blessings brought to us by the Trinity, and of the love and care Christians are called to provide.

Planting an iris garden could also become part of a Habitat for Humanity building project. For this variation, get permission from both the organization and the homeowner to include a small planting of iris on the grounds of the new house.

Iris

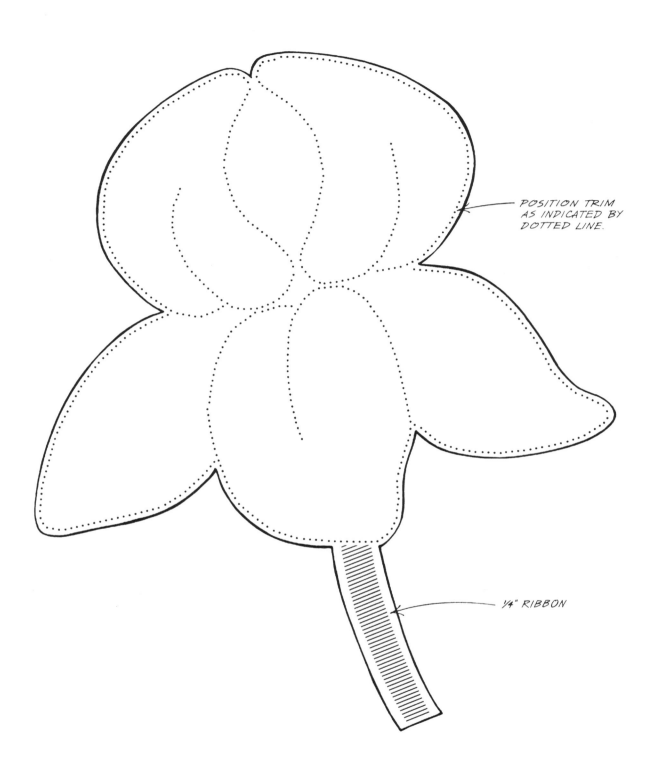

POSITION TRIM
AS INDICATED BY
DOTTED LINE.

¼" RIBBON

Shamrock

The shamrock is called the "Irish Shamrock" because not only is it found growing in Ireland, but one legend says that about four hundred years after Christ a missionary named Patrick (later known as St. Patrick) came before the Irish king and explained the Trinity to him. But this only made the king angry and confused because he could not understand the idea of "three persons in one." Patrick bent down, picked a shamrock, and showed the king that one perfect leaf could have three perfect parts. The king could not explain whether the shamrock was one leaf or three, and that is how he came to understand that something so complex and unbelievable could be true. From that day forward, the shamrock has been a symbol of the Trinity.

Activity: Trinity Coasters

You will need:
   ceramic tiles (plain white is best)
   green permanent felt-tip markers
   felt
   scissors
   glue
   clear adhesive paper
   reduced-size photocopies of the shamrock symbol pattern (optional)

Give each person a tile. Have them use the green permanent markers to draw a shamrock on the tile. (Provide reduced-size photocopies of the shamrock on page 99 for anyone who needs a pattern.) Make sure they completely color in the shamrock. Let the tiles dry long enough so that the marker does not smear. Then have each person cut a piece of clear adhesive paper that will cover the tile completely, top and bottom. After the tiles are covered with clear adhesive paper, glue a square of felt to the bottom of the tile, covering the adhesive paper on this side.

If you wish, you could have your group members write out the story of the Irish Shamrock (or you could type it out beforehand and make copies for everyone). These coasters could be given as gifts along with a copy of the Irish Shamrock legend, or they could be taken home by your group to serve as a constant reminder of the Trinity.

Shamrock

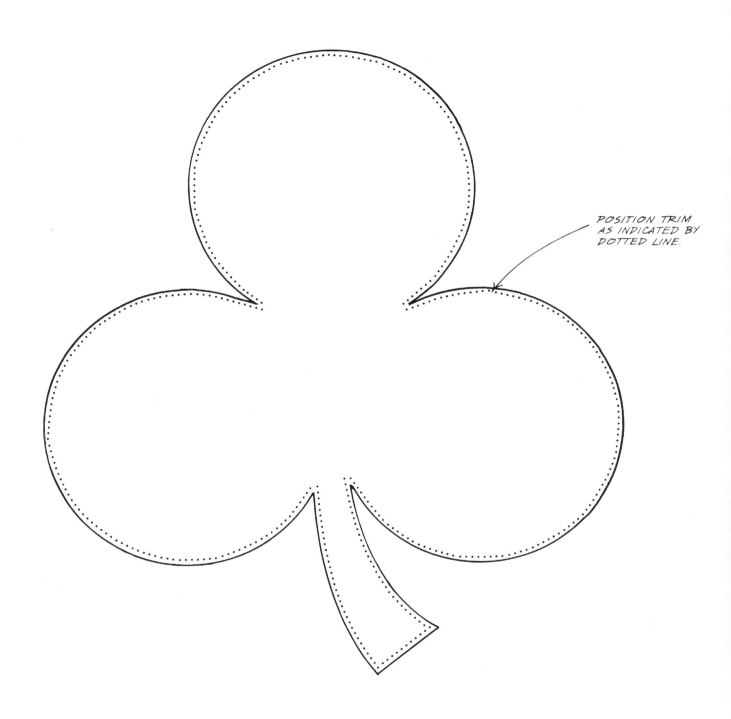

POSITION TRIM
AS INDICATED BY
DOTTED LINE.

Symbols of Faith

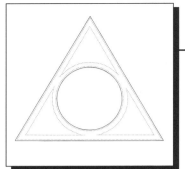

Circle and Triangle

The triangle, with its three points and three angles, is a symbol for the Trinity. The circle (a symbol of eternity) within the triangle represents the eternity of the Trinity.

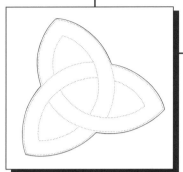

Triquetra

The triquetra is made by placing arcs of several circles together in a design so that the center of the arcs forms a triangle. The arcs are always of equal size, symbolizing the equality of the three parts of the Trinity.

Activity: Keep It Simple

The Trinity is a very difficult concept for most western minds to comprehend. (For some reason, many eastern cultures seem to have less trouble with this concept.) No human explanation of the Trinity is perfect, but it can be the beginning of understanding.

One explanation that most people can grasp on some level is one that uses the three states of water as an example, which can be easily explained or demonstrated. Use this explanation to discuss the Trinity with your group now.

The solid form of water is ice. For Christians this represents Jesus, the member of the Trinity we can see and feel.

The liquid form of water is water. While water can be experienced and seen and felt, it is not experienced in exactly the same way all the time. Water is constant; it is present in almost everything (after all, even humans are made up mostly of water). This form of water represents God. Water falls as rain, runs in rivers, and can be used to quench thirst and to help us make other things. Water is rather difficult to hold in your hand without a container.

The most difficult form of water to see or "get ahold of" is steam. Steam is made when water is heated up. Steam can be seen in only small glimpses. It can be felt if you stand over it or get too close to it. Steam comes from water and does not exist without it. Steam is the form of water that represents the Holy Spirit.

Symbols of Faith

Circle and Triangle

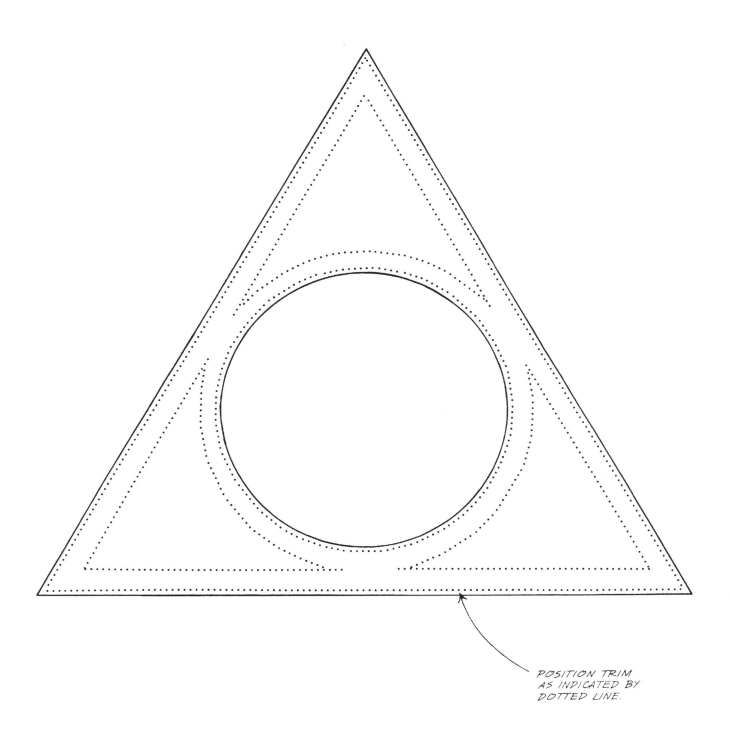

POSITION TRIM
AS INDICATED BY
DOTTED LINE.

Symbols of Faith

Triquetra

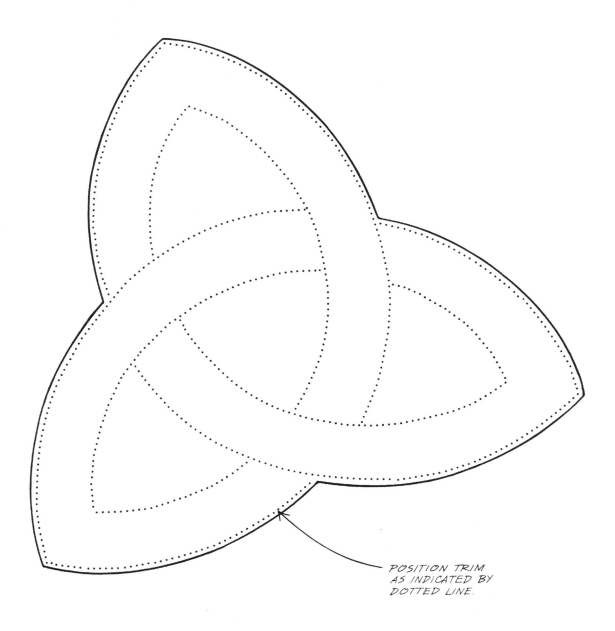

POSITION TRIM
AS INDICATED BY
DOTTED LINE.

Symbols of Faith

General Christian Symbols

Open Bible

The Bible is a symbol for the Word of God. The open Bible tells us that the Bible is for all people.

Activity: open a Book

Books can be a big part of great ways to be of service to others. Here are a few suggestions for book-related service projects:

Read to Someone
Read to a young child or to someone who is ill or could just use some companionship and entertainment. Anyone of any age who is able to read can give of themselves by reading to someone else. The time and attention that goes along with the act of reading to someone is a great demonstration of God's love.

Give Books
Research the book needs of your community. Is there a community center nearby that needs books? Is there a school in your area that could use more books? Organize a book drive to gather books for such an organization and to bring the joy and benefits of reading to as many people as possible.
- Ask everyone in your congregation to "glean" books from their own personal book collections to donate. Be sure that these books are in good condition and are the type of reading that someone would appreciate now.
- Hold a fundraiser and use the money you raise to buy new books to give.
- Contact local bookstores and/or publishers and ask for donations of books.

Help Someone Learn to Read
Younger children need to practice their developing reading skills. Get involved in mentoring a younger child in reading—preteens and youth can be really good at this!

There are many adults who never learned to read and who want to start now. Contact your local adult literacy agency to learn what opportunities are available for your group to help adults learn to read.

Hold a ceremony for your group to declare their specific pledge for the next year to teach someone to read or to help someone learn to enjoy reading. At the end of the year have a party to celebrate your attempts at opening the world of books to others.

Symbols of Faith

Open Bible

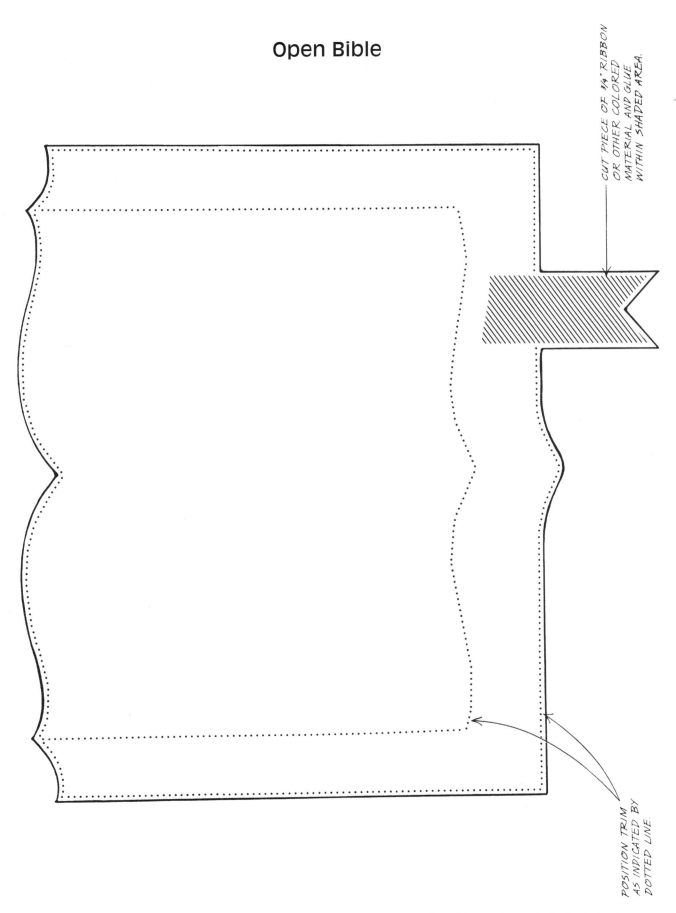

CUT PIECE OF ¾" RIBBON
OR OTHER COLORED
MATERIAL AND GLUE
WITHIN SHADED AREA.

POSITION TRIM
AS INDICATED BY
DOTTED LINE.

Symbols of Faith

Bell

Worship services are good times to step outside of our hectic daily existence and spend a few moments in prayer and contemplation. The importance of this worship time for Christians makes the bell a significant symbol for us. The bell represents calling us forth to worship. It reminds us that we are to take time to set ourselves apart from worldly cares and worship God. The church bell also sends us forth to take the Word of God to the world. Many churches still chime the hours that call us forth to worship, whether with church bells in the tower, a handbell, or a special key on the organ.

Bells make joyous sounds. People around the world ring bells from church towers for weddings and other special occasions. We love to ring bells in celebration at Christmastime and sing songs about bells like "Jingle Bells." Many churches even have handbell choirs.

Activity: Ring Bells

- If you are lucky enough to have a church with a tower and an old-fashioned bell, get permission for your group to take turns ringing the bell on Sunday morning.

- If you have a handbell choir, invite them to come and play for your group. Perhaps they will even let you try a bell or two.

- Create a display of all the bells that you can gather—cowbells, Christmas bells, sleighbells, dinner bells, and so forth. Let everyone try out each type of bell. Ask if they know what each bell is used for. Talk about what each bell sound reminds us of.

Symbols of Faith

Bell

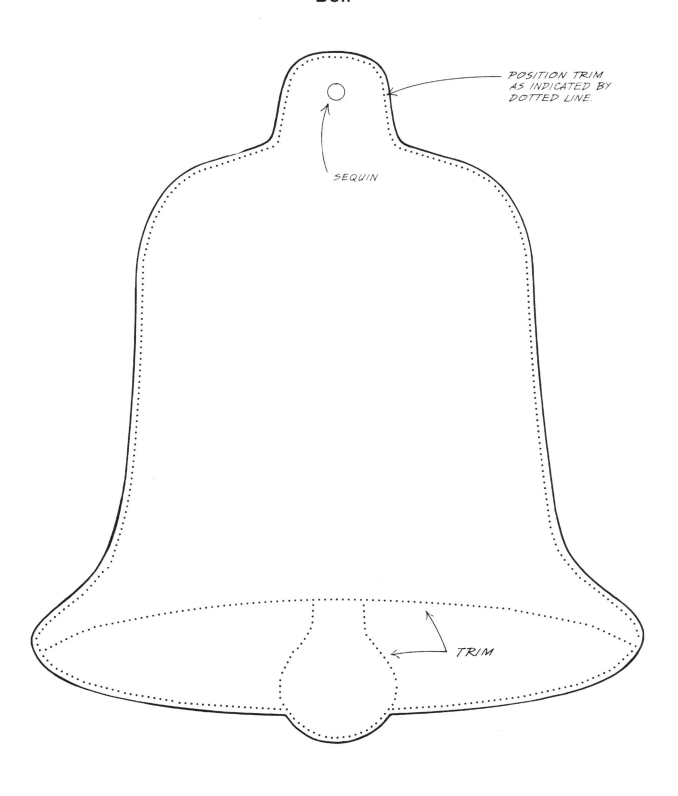

POSITION TRIM
AS INDICATED BY
DOTTED LINE.

SEQUIN

TRIM

Symbols of Faith

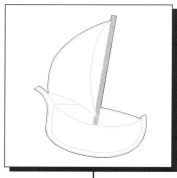

Boat (Ship)

Boats are mentioned in many places in the New Testament. Many of the disciples were called away from their fishing boats to follow Jesus. Once Jesus calmed an angry storm that was tossing around the boat that he and the disciples were in. Another time Jesus walked across water to a boat full of disciples. The disciples who spread the good news from country to country travelled by boat as well as on foot.

The boat (or ship) symbol represents how the church is our refuge in this "rough sea" of life and should remind us to live faithfully as Christ taught us.

Activity: Boat Races

You will need:
> single-serving-sized plastic soda bottles (16 or 20 oz.) with caps
> unsharpened pencils
> duct tape
> white paper
> scissors
> craft knife
> wading pool or access to another shallow body of water

Here are the instructions for making a boat for today's "boat race."

• Tape two pencils lengthwise (one on each side) to a soda bottle to make the body of the boat.
• Fill the bottle about one-third full with water and put the cap back on.
• Use a craft knife to make a small hole on the top side of the bottle, approximately one inch below where the bottle begins to narrow toward the neck (this will be the bow of your boat).
• Tape a 6" square of white paper to the third pencil to make a sail.
• Insert the pencil in the hole in the bottle. Make sure the pencil is straight or your boat will capsize.
• Test your boat for seaworthiness. If it rolls over, then add more water to the bottle.

When everyone has a seaworthy boat, take the group to the wading pool (or other shallow body of water) and point out the starting and finishing points for your boat race. At your signal, teams (or individuals) will race their boats across the water by blowing hard against the sails.

As a variation on this activity, ask each group to create their own boat design using whatever materials they have available. This could even be a group assignment for the week or month between meetings. This way, each group could get together to decide what type of boat to make and then build it for the boat races during your next session.

Symbols of Faith

Boat

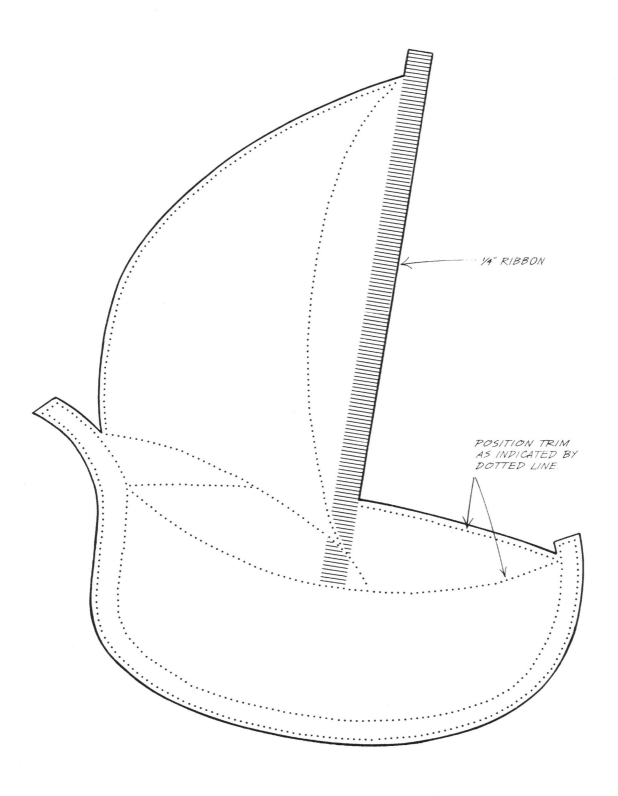

1/4" RIBBON

POSITION TRIM
AS INDICATED BY
DOTTED LINE.

Symbols of Faith

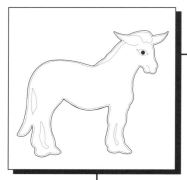

Donkey

The donkey is a symbol associated with both Christmas and Palm Sunday. Because riding a donkey was a basic mode of transportation during Bible times, Christmas scenes often show Mary riding a donkey (a rather uncomfortable arrangement for a pregnant woman) to Bethlehem. Depictions of the flight of Mary and Joseph to Egypt with the baby Jesus also show Mary and the child on a donkey.

On Palm Sunday we usually hear the story of Jesus riding triumphantly into Jerusalem on a donkey. Jesus told the disciples, "You will find a donkey tied, and a colt with her; untie them and bring them to me" (Matthew 21:2). This scripture is often related to the Old Testament passage about the Messiah found in Zechariah 9:9, "Lo, your king comes to you; triumphant and victorious is he, humble and riding on a donkey, on a colt, the foal of a donkey."

Activity: Sculpt Clay Symbols

You will need:
   self-drying clay
   paints and paintbrushes (optional)

This activity can be done individually, in pairs, or in larger groups.

Give each person, pair, or group a lump of self-drying clay and ask them to sculpt a symbol—it's your choice as to whether they should sculpt specific symbols that go along with today's lesson or if they can choose which symbol they'd like to sculpt.

These sculptures can either be freestanding symbols or made into medallions, wall hangings, oil lamps, and so forth. For a Christmas activity you could divide up the group to make different figures for a clay nativity set, including a clay "cave," since Jesus was probably born in a cave that was used as a stable (a typical stable at that time).

Once the clay symbols have dried (set them aside at least overnight), they may be painted. Or, you can leave the symbols in their natural clay-colored state.

Donkey

Symbols of Faith

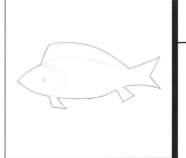

Fish

In the early days of the Christian church the Roman empire ruled much of the world. The Romans saw other religions, like Christianity, as dangerous to the state so they persecuted these other religions. The Christians tried to protect themselves by meeting in secret. One way Christians could communicate secretly with each other (and thus avoid arrest) was by drawing the symbol of the fish. Since fish was a food staple of the time as well as a very important commodity, this symbol could be used by Christians without arousing suspicion.

Christians chose the fish as a symbol because not only were many of Jesus' disciples fishermen, but ICHTHUS, the Greek word for fish, is also an acrostic that uses the first letters of the Greek words that mean Jesus Christ, Son of God, Savior.

Activity: Scripture Fish Wall

You will need:
- Bibles
- concordance or index cards
- crayons, pens, or felt-tip markers
- paper punch and string or yarn (optional)
- netting
- photocopies of fish pattern
- tape

If you do not have a concordance available for your group to use, then borrow one before the group meets and write down New Testament references for verses containing the words *fish, fish's, fishermen, fishes, fishhook, or fishing* (such as Matthew 4:19) on a series of index cards (one reference per card).

If you have a concordance available, let each group look up and choose their own verse about fish.

For this activity, tape netting material to the wall to make a large net.

Divide the group into teams of two, three, or four. Give each team one or more copies of the fish pattern and pens, crayons, or felt-tip markers. Ask each group to find a New Testament fish reference in the concordance (or choose an index card from the set you have prepared), look up that Bible verse, and then write the verse on the fish (along with the reference). Let them decorate their fish any way they like. When they've finished, have them tape their fish to the net. Or, they could punch a hole in each fish, run a piece of yarn through, and tie it to the net.

Another option for this activity would be to let the group make a net by tying together pieces of string. Lay out several long pieces of string parallel to each other, then lay shorter pieces of string across the first set. Knot the ends of the short string to the long strings, forming little squares until you create a large net. (There are other methods for making your own net—you may want to enlist the help of a few creative people for this symbol project.)

Fish

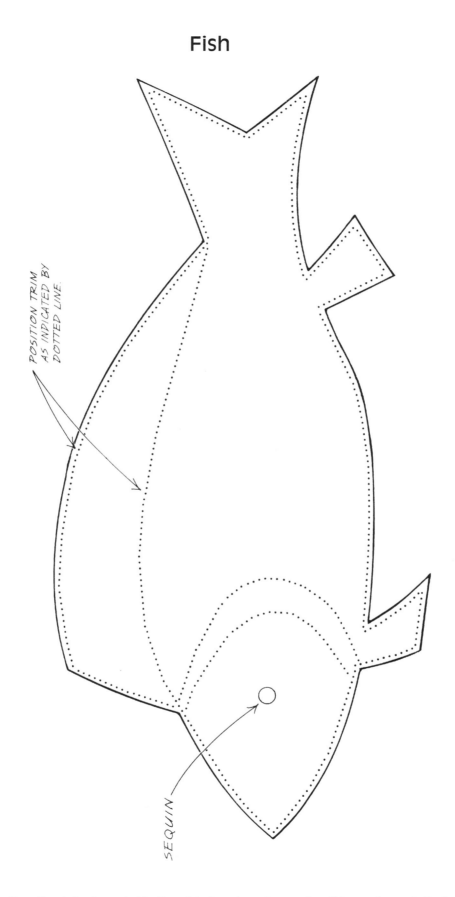

POSITION TRIM AS INDICATED BY DOTTED LINE.

SEQUIN

Lamp

The lamp represents the Bible, the Word of God. Light symbolizes knowledge and learning and reminds us how the Word of God sheds light on our lives. A primitive-looking oil lamp, one of the oldest kinds of lamp we know of, is usually used to represent the Word of God—remember, the Word of God has been around since Creation and still lights our way today.

The lamp symbol probably comes from Psalm 119:105, "Your word is a lamp to my feet and a light to my path."

Activity: "Light Unto the World" Altar

You will need:
  table
  tablecloth or altar cloth
  various sources of light

Prepare an altar for your own worship center or ask your church office for permission to decorate the altar in the church sanctuary as a "Light Unto the World" altar for Christian Education Sunday or a similar promotional event.

Ask the group members to bring various (and hopefully interesting) sources of light to put on the altar, such as lava lamps, desk lamps, candles, flashlights, lanterns, floor lamps, tap lights, nightlights, and old oil lamps.

Cover the altar or table with a cloth. Place the sources of light both on and around the altar. Light the candles, a few of the lamps (the number you can light will depend on how many electrical outlets near the altar there are), and perhaps a flashlight. (It's probably not a good idea to light a lantern indoors.) Take time to discuss as a group how Christians are called to be a light unto the world by spreading God's Word.

Symbols of Faith

Lamp

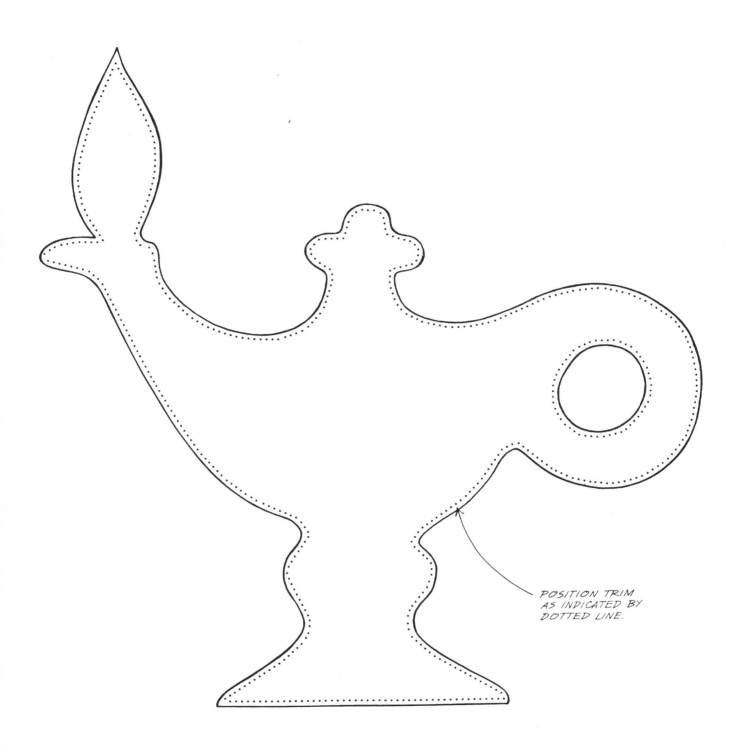

POSITION TRIM
AS INDICATED BY
DOTTED LINE.

Symbols of Faith

Sheep (Lamb)

Sheep can symbolize numerous things. Sheep are often used to represent people. "We are his people, and the sheep of his pasture" (Psalm 100:3c). When Jesus is called the Good Shepherd—"I am the good shepherd. The good shepherd lays down his life for the sheep" (John 10:11)—we are his sheep. Many of the Psalms also use this same image of people as sheep who belong to God.

When we talk about the Lamb we are usually referring to Jesus. The lamb is a symbol of sacrifice. The story of the Hebrews' escape from Egypt talks about the Hebrews sprinkling the blood of the lamb on their doorposts as protection. Jesus himself is often called the "Lamb" who was "sacrificed" for us.

Activity: Bible Bookmark

You will need:
- construction paper
- clear adhesive paper
- reduced-size photocopies of symbol patterns
- markers, colored pencils, or crayons
- yarn or colored ribbon
- scissors
- ruler
- paper punch
- dried or plastic flowers or other small, flat, interesting items and glue

Choose several of the symbol patterns you would like to use and make reduced-size photocopies of these patterns, small enough to fit on a bookmark (approximately 1½" wide).

Have each member of your group measure and cut out the construction paper they will be using for the main part of the bookmark. (A good size for this is 1½" wide and 6"-7" long.) Have everyone do the same with the clear adhesive paper (each bookmark will need two pieces of the clear adhesive paper) BUT be sure to cut the clear adhesive paper at least ¼"-½" longer and wider than the construction paper.

After everyone has cut out pieces of construction paper and clear adhesive paper, ask them to use the patterns you have photocopied to outline a symbol on their bookmark. They may color the symbol and decorate the paper any way they like—they could even copy a short Bible verse onto the bookmark.

When the group has finished decorating their bookmarks, have them each place one of the pieces of clear adhesive paper on the table, sticky side up, carefully position the decorated construction paper strip in the center of the adhesive strip, and place it on the adhesive. Then they should very carefully align the other piece of clear adhesive paper, sticky side down, on top of the construction paper. Ask everyone to press the three layers together firmly and trim any overlapping edges with scissors. Then punch a hole in the top of each bookmark, thread a piece yarn or ribbon through the hole, and tie it securely.

Suggest that they use these bookmarks to mark their place in their personal Bibles.

Sheep

SEQUIN

LOOP TRIM TO CREATE
A CURLY EFFECT

POSITION TRIM
AS INDICATED BY
DOTTED LINE.

Symbols of Faith

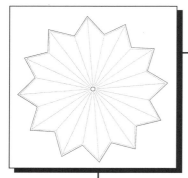

Twelve-Pointed Star

The number twelve has always been an important number in the Bible, and stands for God's closeness to people. The twelve-pointed star has two specific meanings. It represents the twelve tribes of Israel, and it also symbolizes the twelve disciples.

Activity: Make Symbol Puzzles

You will need:
    several photocopies of the puzzle grid on page 48
    pencils

Be sure to make several photocopies of the blank puzzle grid because it usually takes several tries to line up a puzzle in exactly the way you desire.

Make a list of the words that you plan to include in your word search or crossword puzzle, then organize the words by their length. This is important in creating either type of puzzle.

When your puzzle is complete, make photocopies of the finished puzzle, give one to each member of your group, and let everyone work them either in groups or individually.

Word Search

Start with your longest words at one corner of your puzzle. Words in a word search can go right to left, left to right, up, down, across, or diagonally; the words may cross each other by sharing a common letter or not touch at all. You will not need to provide clues for a word search, but be sure to post a list of the words hidden in the puzzle.

Crossword Puzzle

Start in the middle of the grid with a word that has lots of letters in common with other words. Start adding other words, working both upward and downward from the first word. Then start fitting other words that read from left to right into the puzzle. (Be prepared to discard some words if they absolutely don't fit your growing puzzle.) When your crossword puzzle is complete, make a list of clues for both "down" and "across" words.

For a variation of this activity, give your group several copies of the puzzle grid, pencils, and a list of possible symbols—or just give the group a topic and let them decide upon the related symbols to use—and then let them create their own puzzles. This can be an individual or a group activity.

Note: There are also several programs available on the Internet that you can use to build your own puzzle on your computer.

Twelve-Pointed Star

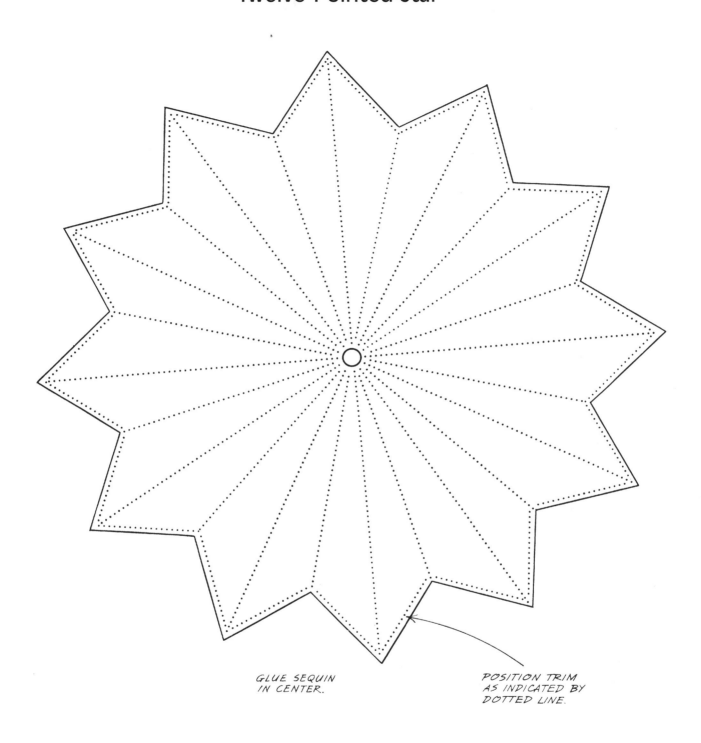

GLUE SEQUIN
IN CENTER.

POSITION TRIM
AS INDICATED BY
DOTTED LINE.

Burning Torch

The burning torch symbolizes the Christian call to witness to the world. The torch reminds us of Jesus' words in Matthew 5:14, "you are the light of the world," and in Matthew 5:16, "let your light shine before others, so that they may see your good works and give glory to your Father in heaven."

We are familiar with the tradition of Greek relay races in which each runner passes the torch to another runner, much like the Olympic torch is handed off today. Just as runners in a race pass the torch, each generation of Christians passes the Christian faith to another generation.

Activity: Pass the Torch

You will need:
> flashlights or "torches" made from paper towel rolls, aluminum foil, red construction paper, and tape
> index cards
> pen

Use this activity to help your group remember the Bible verse, "I have fought the good fight, I have finished the race, I have kept the faith" (2 Timothy 4:7).

Before the group meets, make a set of Bible verse cards for as many teams as you anticipate having for this activity. Each set of cards should consist of sixteen index cards, with one word of 2 Timothy 4:7 written on each.

Set up an obstacle course in a large room or an open area outdoors. Make the course challenging without being overwhelming to persons of all ages and physical abilities. If you have anyone in your group for whom any sort of running (or even fast walking) is a problem, give everyone the choice of handing the torch off to a surrogate runner, or allow these people to skip the most difficult obstacles or to have assistance through parts of the course. Station people at different locations around the course to hand Bible verse index cards to the runners. Supply enough flashlights for each group; or, as a craft activity, have each group make their own torch out of a paper towel roll, aluminum foil, and red construction paper.

At your signal, the first runners for each group will start around the course. They are to run the course to the point where they are handed one of the words to the Bible verse, then run back to their group and hand off the torch to the next runner. This should continue until each group has accumulated all of the words to 2 Timothy 4:7 and put the Bible verse in order. THERE ARE NO LOSERS IN THIS GAME! Every group finishes the race and keeps the faith.

Burning Torch

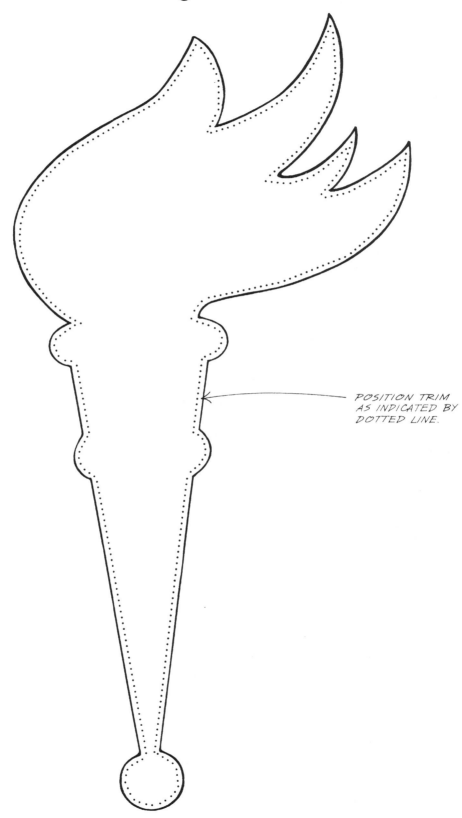

POSITION TRIM
AS INDICATED BY
DOTTED LINE.

Symbols of Faith

Activity: Symbols Review Games

You will need (depending on the game you choose):

Bible	posterboard
index cards	felt-tip markers
pens	timer
buzzer or bell	tape

Use the information you have gathered about symbols to devise a fun review game. There are endless ways to do this. (However, to avoid any individual embarrassment or stress and to foster a spirit of teamwork, have your group members work in teams and ask them to always give ONE answer that has been decided upon by the team.)

1. A *Jeopardy!* type game can serve as a great review of quite a few symbols in different categories. Divide a large sheet of posterboard into five categories across the top, with five spaces under each heading—for example: Christmas, Easter, New Testament, Old Testament, and Other Special Days.

   Write the points on index cards—100, 200, 300, 400, and 500 for each category—and tape the cards to the posterboard. You do not need to write the questions on the board; just have them on hand (organized by category and points) to read aloud. In order to keep track of which questions have been answered, simply remove the index card for that point number and category.

2. The "Who Wants to Be a Millionaire?" style is popular. Just come up with a number of multiple-choice questions to ask.

3. The "Wheel of Fortune" model involves putting different letters on index cards and posting the index cards (letter side hidden) on the wall. Rearrange the letters for the name of each different symbol, and let groups keep guessing letters until one manages to guess the word.

4. "Ring the Bell"—You ask a question; the teams are given a chance to discuss possible answers; and when a team has decided on an answer, they ring a bell (or press a buzzer) and are given a chance to answer. If the first team is wrong, the next team gets a chance to answer.

5. "Hangman"—Pick a symbol and draw spaces for the number of letters in the name of the symbol. The teams must guess letters to fill the blanks, racing to guess the symbol before you complete drawing a picture (for each wrong letter they guess, draw another line to the picture). (The hangman image may be too violent, so draw a flower or something else that will take several strokes to finish.)

6. "Baseball"—Set up a baseball diamond, and for every question answered correctly the team "at bat" will advance around the bases to home. There are several variations on this—pick one you like.

7. Be creative—make up your own game!

Old Testament Symbols

Ark and Rainbow

The ark and the rainbow are the most common symbols of the Flood and may be used together or separately. This symbol represents the church, because all living creatures found a safe refuge on the ark (just as all people are welcomed into the body of Christ). The rainbow by itself is a symbol of God's continuing love for all creation and of God's covenant with Noah.

Activity: Flood Relief

God promised that the whole earth would never again be destroyed by a flood, but God did not promise that there would never again be floods on the earth.

Before today's meeting, you will need to obtain a list of supplies your group can gather to help with flood relief. These lists are readily available from local or national relief agencies, or from your denomination's national headquarters.

The Red Cross and similar programs mainly take financial donations, so you could plan a fundraiser to raise money for one of these organizations. Use creative ideas such as making an ark to collect the money in, or advertising your campaign while wearing big rubber boots and raincoats. Let your group decide what their goal will be and how they want to raise the money, and be sure to set a time limit to do this in.

Some organizations such as the United Methodist Committee on Relief (UMCOR) also accept donations of materials. You may donate "kits" such as a "flood bucket" filled with materials needed for flood relief. The list of materials needed for a flood bucket can be found on the UMCOR website at http://gbgm-umc.org/umcor/kits.html or by contacting the UMCOR Depot, P.O. Box 850, 131 Sager Brown Road, Baldwin, LA 70514-0850.

Ark and Rainbow

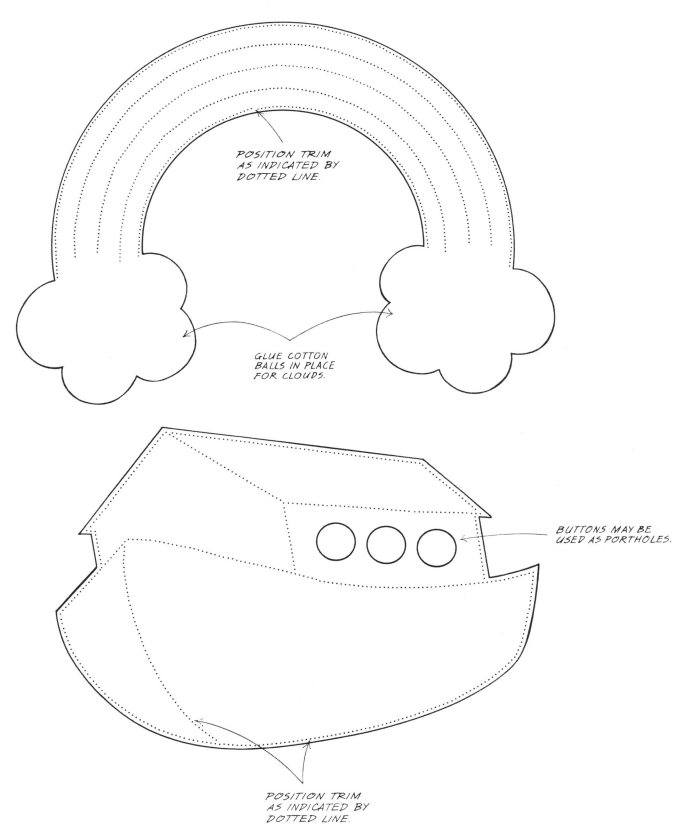

POSITION TRIM
AS INDICATED BY
DOTTED LINE.

GLUE COTTON
BALLS IN PLACE
FOR CLOUDS.

BUTTONS MAY BE
USED AS PORTHOLES.

POSITION TRIM
AS INDICATED BY
DOTTED LINE.

Burning Bush

The bush that burned but was not consumed by the flames (see Exodus 3:2) is the symbol of the adult Moses. (A basket nestled in bullrushes symbolizes the baby Moses.) The burning bush reminds us of the dramatic call Moses received from God to lead the Israelites from Egypt.

Activity: Burning Bush Animation

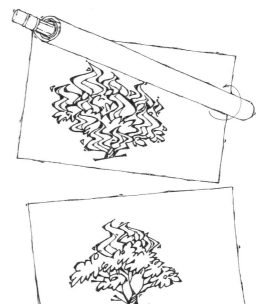

You will need:
    8½"-by-11" sheets of white paper
    scissors
    pencils
    markers or pens

With this activity you can make a very simple animated picture that shows the bush "burn" but not be consumed.

1. Fold a piece of 8½"-by-11" white paper in half and cut the paper along the crease. Fold one of these halves in half again so that it looks like a simple greeting card.

2. Draw a picture of a burning bush on the bottom of the front page. Draw a very similar picture with a few variations on the bottom of the inside page. The small differences between the two pictures are what create the illusion of movement. For example, the burning bush on the front page may have four tongues of fire very close together coming out of the bush and almost covering the bush; while the bush on the inside page may be more exposed with only three tongues of fire rising up, widely spread apart.

3. Roll the top picture tightly around a pencil all the way to the left (toward the crease). This will make the first page curl. Release the curled paper.

4. Set the picture on a flat surface and use the pencil to rub the curled first page back and forth over the inside page to "animate" the picture. If you do this quickly enough you should be able to see the bush "burn."

Note: It takes at least two separate pictures to make an animation. However, if you have enough time you can add more layers of pictures, each one slightly different from the one before. For longer animations like this it might be better to create a small "book" of folded papers and, holding the creased side in one hand, flip through the pages to see the picture animate.

Symbols of Faith

Burning Bush

Symbols of Faith

Dove with Olive Sprig

The dove with the olive sprig is often used as a symbol of the Flood. It represents peace, forgiveness, and the anticipation of new life. The dove returned to the ark with an olive sprig in its beak, which signalled to Noah that the worst was over and the earth would live again.

This dove is also often used as a symbol of peace, and should not be confused with the descending dove, a symbol of the Holy Spirit.

Activity: Work for Peace

For this activity you will need to gather information on local, national, and international organizations that work for peace. Choose one of these and find ways that your group can interact with this organization (by writing letters, attending rallies, organizing fundraisers, and so forth).

Two possible organizations to look into are listed below.

Sadako Peace Project for Children
P. O. Box 1253
Issaquah, WA 98027-1253
www.sadako.org

Sadako was a young Japanese girl who developed leukemia after the atomic bomb was dropped on Hiroshima, Japan, at the end of World War II. This organization tells Sadako's story and provides opportunities for children to be involved in the work toward peace, including a link for children who would like a pen pal who is interested in world peace.

The Carter Center
453 Freedom Parkway
Atlanta, Ga 30307
www.cartercenter.org

Take a look at the "Waging Peace" section.

Dove With Olive Sprig

SEQUIN

POSITION TRIM
AS INDICATED BY
DOTTED LINE.

¹⁄₁₆" RIBBON

Harp

The harp (lyre) represents praise and worship. King David, who is credited with writing many of the Psalms, played a harp. Psalms are still used in worship today. "I will go to the altar of God, to God my exceeding joy; and I will praise you with the harp, O God, my God" (Psalm 43:4). The harp makes a wonderful symbol for a choir.

Activity: Play Musical Instruments

(for the "musically challenged")

For this activity you will need musical instruments of any variety: "real" musical instruments; musical instruments you can make as crafts; pieces of wood to strike together; pan lids and spoons; a jar full of beans; a tabletop and a pair of hands; glasses with different levels of water and spoons; and so forth.

"Make a joyful noise to the LORD, all the earth. Worship the LORD with gladness; come into his presence with singing." (Psalm 100:1)

NO MUSICAL TALENT IS REQUIRED. However, if anyone in your group is musically talented, ask them to bring their instruments with them today. If there are any people with absolutely NO musical abilities, don't worry! They can still participate and enjoy today's activity. Anything you can find or make that you can use to make noise or pound out a simple rhythm will work. Just remember, the object of today's music is joyful noise and sounds of praise to God, not a beautiful sound.

Designate someone who can play the piano or who has an ear for rhythm and can lead the group to get everyone ready to use their instruments. Let everyone practice "playing" their "instrument" to the beat. Have fun with this. Anyone at any age—from the very young to the very old—can make a "joyful noise." The more laughter and fun your group shares, the better.

Symbols of Faith

Harp

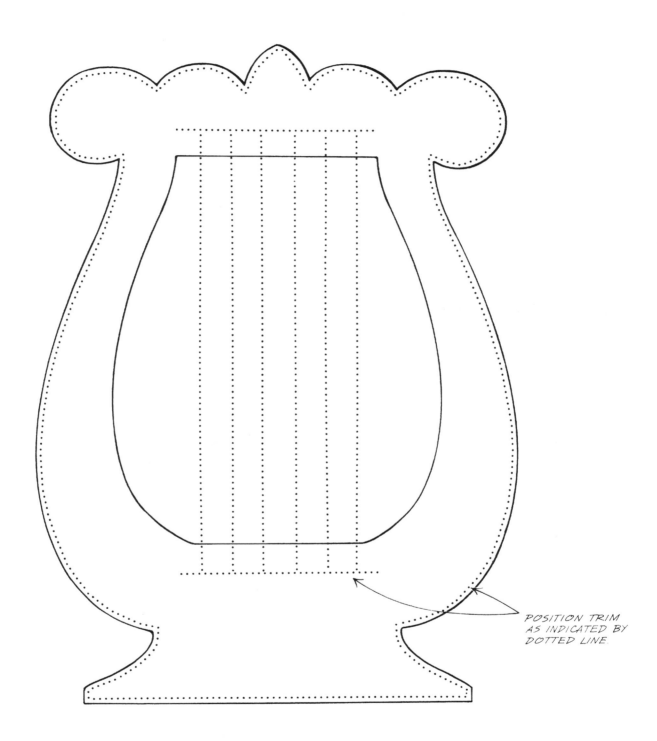

POSITION TRIM
AS INDICATED BY
DOTTED LINE.

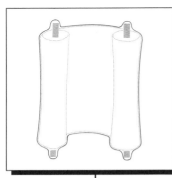

Scroll

The scroll represents the Torah, or the five books of the law of Moses. Christians refer to these as the first five books of the Old Testament. The laws of God represented in these scrolls were sacred to the Jews. Though Christians do not follow the strict dietary and worship laws found in the Torah, we do have great respect for these laws, especially the Ten Commandments.

Activity: The Perfect Scroll

You will need:
    Bibles
    paper
    pens

When a scribe wrote Scripture by hand onto a scroll, it had to be perfect. If a scribe made a mistake, he had to start completely over on a new piece of parchment. This practice still holds true today. The Torah used in Jewish temples and synagogues is copied by hand onto scrolls and no mistakes are allowed. Try this with your group. It's not as easy as you might think.

Assign each member of your group a very lengthy piece of scripture to copy. They must copy it exactly—spelling, punctuation, *everything* must be exact. If anyone makes a mistake, he or she must start completely over on a new sheet of paper. Use pens for this activity so that no one is tempted to erase any mistakes.

This might become very frustrating for a lot of people. But this frustration is exactly what you wish everyone to understand. This activity will help them become aware of the care and diligence required to undertake a task such as this. It should also impress upon them how important this task is considered. After all, this is Scripture.

You will probably have to end this activity before most people have finished. That's okay because the process, not the finished product, is the object.

Hold a debriefing session after everyone has tried this in order to let the group express how they felt. How easy did they find this task? How difficult was it? Why is this process so important? What does it mean in today's world of computers and fast *everything* that people still take the time to write the sacred Scriptures by hand and do it perfectly?

Note: Be sure to recycle the discarded papers.

Symbols of Faith

Scroll

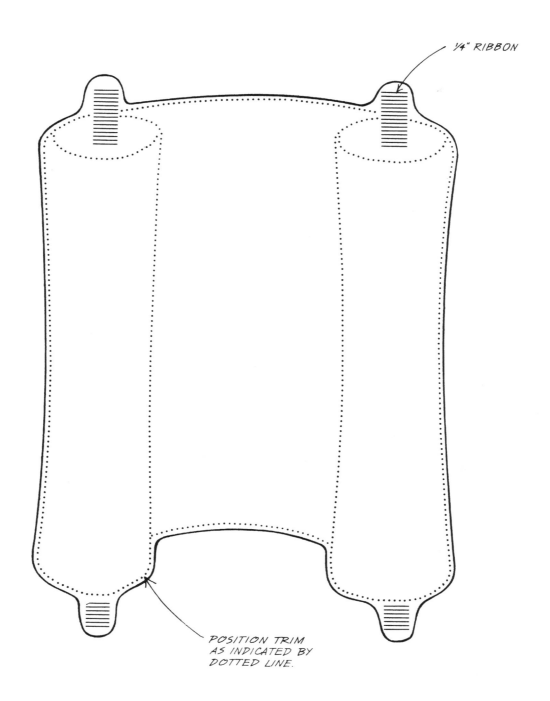

¼" RIBBON

POSITION TRIM
AS INDICATED BY
DOTTED LINE.

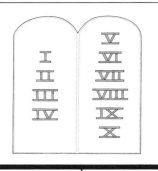

Stone Tablets

This symbol is usually shown as two stone tablets side by side with four letters on one side and six on the other. These stone tablets represent the Ten Commandments given to Moses by God. The four numbers on one side represent the first four commandments, which deal with our relationship with God. The other six numbers represent the last six commandments, which deal with our relationships with each other.

Activity:
Commandments from Another Side

You will need:
Bibles
paper
pencils

Divide your group into teams. Have each team look in the Bible at the Ten Commandments, Exodus 20:1-17. (If they would like to see another listing of the Ten Commandments, have them look at Deuteronomy 5:1-22.)

To make this activity more like a game, set a time limit of approximately 15 to 20 minutes for the teams to work. After everyone is finished, bring the group back together to compare notes.

THE TASK (you can do either the first option or the second, or both, or assign different options to different teams):

1. Have each team look at the Ten Commandments and rewrite them in a way that means the same thing but uses the opposite approach. For example, "Honor your father and mother" might become "You shall not speak to your parents disrespectfully." "You shall not kill" might become "You shall have respect for all human life and treat others as you would want to be treated."

2. Look at each commandment one by one and write specific examples of ways to keep each commandment.

Stone Tablets

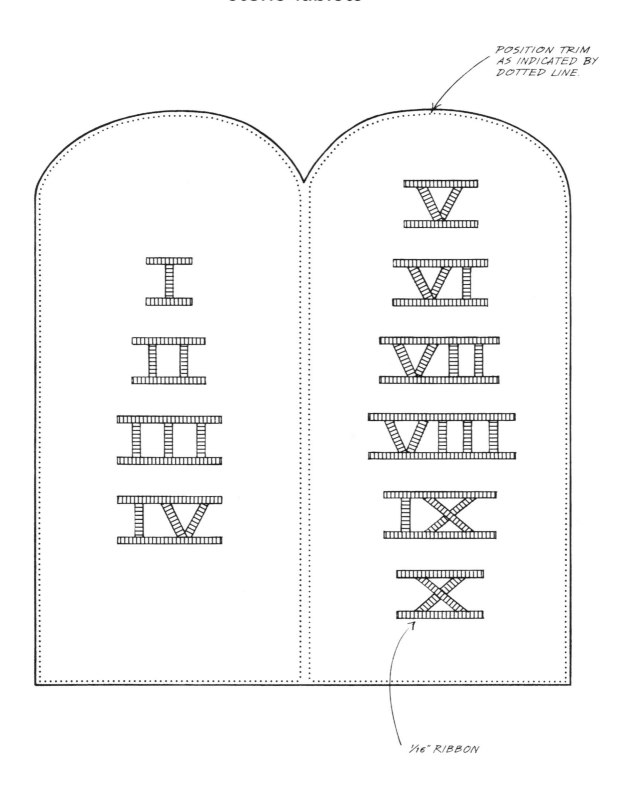

POSITION TRIM
AS INDICATED BY
DOTTED LINE.

1/16" RIBBON

Symbols of Faith

Tent

The tent is an Old Testament symbol often used to represent Abraham, who lived a nomadic life in a tent. Abraham followed God's call and went where God led. The tent is used as a symbol of the willingness to follow where God calls.

Activity: Set Up and Take Down Camp

You will need:
> tent
> camping equipment
> food
> pets
> outdoor setting

This activity is a symbolic way of experiencing just how daunting it would be to take everything you own and move to a new place. To really get into the spirit of things, make sure there is lots of equipment such as a tent, a dining setup, sleeping bags and pillows, food and food preparation supplies, lanterns, supplies for cleaning up after meals, a throw rug for the floor of the tent (yes, Abraham and Sarah would have had rugs in their tents!), and so forth. Don't forget things such as lawn chairs and pets (Sarah and Abraham had livestock to worry about). The more challenging the job of putting up and taking down the tent is, the more this lifestyle will be understood and appreciated.

Have your group set up a complete campsite as if they were going to be there for a full weekend of camping. When you're all set up, prepare and eat a meal. (Don't forget to feed the pets!) Immediately after the meal, take down the camp and pack all of the supplies away.

Discuss how difficult this type of lifestyle must have been. Yes, Abraham and Sarah often stayed in one place longer than a weekend, but each time they moved on they had to move EVERYTHING they owned.

Tent

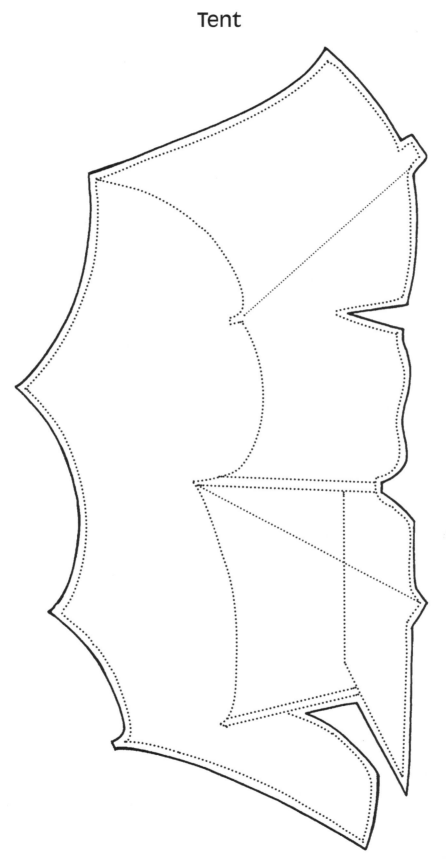

Activity: Designing Logos

DESIGN AN INDIVIDUAL DISCIPLE SHIELD
You will need:
> pencils
> felt-tip markers or crayons
> photocopies of the blank shield pattern (page 151)

As a group, review that a symbol is an object (something we can see) that stands for something else (often an idea or quality that we can't see). Most symbols are created because they mean something special to the people who choose to use that particular symbol.

Even though everyone will be designing his or her own individual symbol, let them work in groups to discuss and decide upon symbols to use.

Ask each group to think of one thing about themselves that represents what they are like as Christian disciples. What one word or phrase would they use to describe themselves? (Think of things like *missionary, storyteller, helper, cook,* or *singer of praise to God.*) The group can help each individual member identify talents he or she has that he or she can use to spread the Word of God. (Remember, children can be active Christian disciples and already have gifts of their own to offer.) Then ask each person to decide upon a symbol for the word or phrase they came up with that describes what they can offer in the spirit of Christian discipleship.

Give each person a photocopy of the blank disciple shield (page 151) and markers or crayons. (They might want to sketch their symbol in pencil first, so have a supply on hand.) Ask everyone to use the symbol they decided upon to make their own Disciple Shield. When the shields are complete, everyone can take them home to serve as a reminder of the work they can do for God.

DESIGN A GROUP SHIELD OR LOGO
You will need:
> pencils
> felt-tip markers or crayons
> paper
> posterboard
> photocopies of blank shield pattern (page 151)

Discuss with your group how Christian symbols and the Disciple Shields can perform the same function as today's familiar company or sports logos. Ask the group, What do you think of when you see (or hear about) the "golden arches"? The (Nike) "swoosh"? What about the group of five different-colored interlocking circles? These circles are the sign of the Olympics and almost anyone who watches sports can tell you immediately what they are when they see them.

Together come to some consensus about what it is you want other people to know about your group or organization. Use this concept to design a logo for your group (again, you could break into smaller teams to decide on a symbol for each team and then come back together to use each symbol in a large group logo). You could take this logo and have it made into t-shirts for your group members if you like, or just work together to make a poster of your logo and hang it somewhere for others to see.

Disciple
Shields

SIMON PETER

Simon Peter, son of Jonah and brother of Andrew, is the most well-known of the twelve original disciples. Jesus gave Simon the name *rock,* from the Aramaic word *cephas.* The Greek version of *cephas* was *petros,* and it is from this Greek word that we get the name *Peter.* Peter became the "rock" upon which the early church was built.

Rock really seems to be a strange name for Peter, since the whole time Jesus knew Peter, Peter kept changing his position. Sometimes Peter's faith in Jesus was there for all to see; at other times Peter's lack of faith was all too evident. He denied Jesus three times the night Jesus was arrested. When Jesus asked Peter to come to him over the water, Peter started to sink because his trust was not complete.

Yet Jesus knew Peter's heart. After Jesus' death, Peter became a solid "rock" and never again wavered in his faith.

Peter's shield displays two crossed keys and an inverted (upside down) cross. The keys on the shield refer to Jesus' statement about Peter being entrusted with the "keys of the kingdom of heaven." The upside down cross refers to the way Peter died. He was crucified upside down because he did not feel worthy of dying in the same way that Jesus had.

Some Bible references for Peter include

Matthew 4:18; 10:1-4; 16:16-19; 17:1-8   John 21:15-19
Mark 1:29; 3:16-19; 9:2; 13:3-4   Acts 1:12-14; 2:14—3:21
Luke 6:12-16

Symbols of Faith

ANDREW

Andrew was Simon Peter's brother. Together they spent their time working as fishermen. In Greek *Andrew* means "manly." Andrew is thought to have been a disciple of John the Baptist, who told Andrew about Jesus. Andrew then introduced his brother, Simon Peter, to Jesus. In fact, Andrew is remembered for his great role in bringing others to Jesus.

Andrew's shield displays an X-shaped cross. Tradition has it that Andrew died a martyr's death in Greece. It is said that Andrew died on an X-shaped cross at his own request because he felt unworthy to die on the same kind of cross that Jesus had died on.

Some Bible references for Andrew include
    Matthew 4:18; 10:1-4
    Mark 1:29; 3:16-19; 13:3-4
    Luke 6:12-16
    John 1:35-42
    Acts 1:12-14

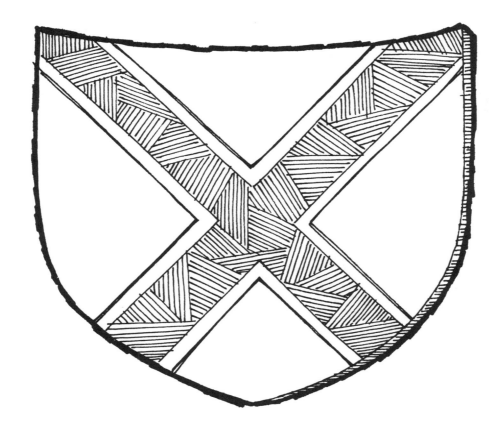

BARTHOLOMEW

(Nathanael)

Bartholomew and Nathanael are usually thought to be the same person. *Bartholomew* is a "patronymic" (what we would call a "last name"). The name *Nathanael* means "gift of God." Nathanael was skeptical of Jesus when they first met until Jesus told Nathanael a lot of things about Nathanael that Jesus should have had no way of knowing, which definitely impressed Nathanael.

Tradition tells us that Bartholomew (Nathanael) traveled extensively on missionary journeys to places such as Egypt, Persia, India, and Armenia. Tradition also tells us that Bartholomew was put to death (by being flayed alive with knives) in Armenia.

Bartholomew's shield displays either one or three knives, signifying his manner of death.

Some Bible references for Bartholomew include
    Matthew 10:1-4
    Mark 3:16-19
    Luke 6:12-16
    John 1:45-51; 21:1-3
    Acts 1:12-14

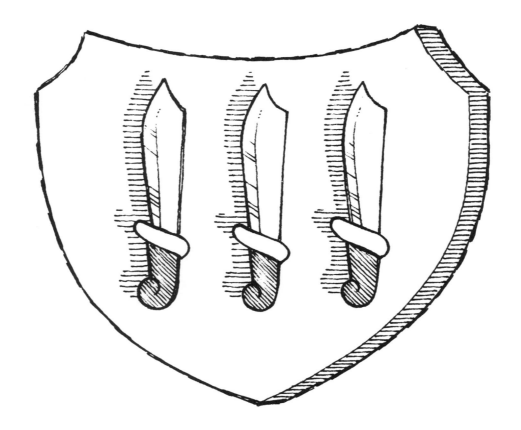

Symbols of Faith

JAMES
(the greater)

James (the greater) was one of the sons of Zebedee—brother of John, the beloved disciple. James, his brother John, and Peter formed the inner circle of Jesus' disciples and were often with Jesus even when the other disciples were absent. The two brothers were nicknamed "Sons of Thunder." Many people believe that this means that they had rather volatile tempers. James is most often referred to in the New Testament along with his brother and/or with Peter. Very little is known about James the greater.

James was the first of the disciples to be martyred for his faith. (Acts 12:1-2). (Remember, Judas Iscariot died by his own hand, he was not martyred.)

James's shield displays three scalloped shells, which stand for James's great missionary work.

Some Bible references for James the greater include
    Matthew 10:1-4
    Mark 1:29; 3:16-19; 9:2; 10:35-45; 13:3-4
    Luke 6:12-16
    Acts 1:12-14

Symbols of Faith

JAMES, SON OF ALPHAEUS

(the younger, or the little)

James, son of Alphaeus, was also known as James the younger (see Mark 15:40) or James the little. He was probably shorter than James the greater, and that is why he is called "the younger" or "the little." He is believed to be the son of the woman named Mary who was at the cross with Mary the mother of Jesus and who was also a witness to the Resurrection.

James the younger's shield displays a saw because tradition tells us that James was martyred when he was thrown from the top of a church. His enemies were so filled with hate that after the fall killed James, they sawed his body into pieces.

Some Bible references for James, son of Alphaeus, include
    Matthew 10:1-4, 27:56
    Mark 3:16-19; 16:1
    Luke 6:12-16, 24:10
    Acts 1:12-14

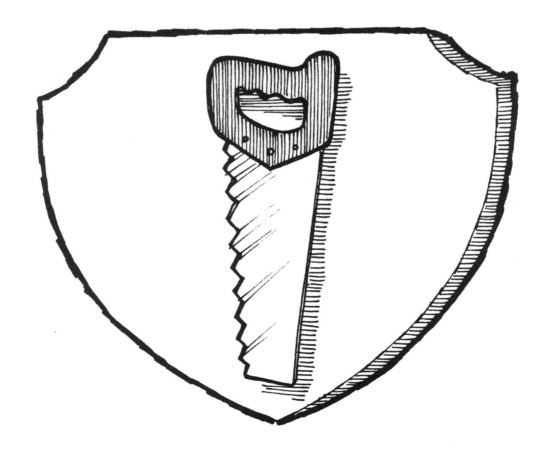

Symbols of Faith

JUDAS, SON OF JAMES

(Thaddeus)

There is little that is known about this Judas. In Luke's Gospel he is called "Judas, son of James." In the book of Mark, this Judas is called Thaddeus; and in some older texts, he is called Lebbeus. Therefore different lists of the disciples are sometimes made up of different names.

Tradition has it that Judas, son of James, (Thaddeus) traveled extensively on missionary journeys that took the good news to many countries. Therefore his disciple shield displays a ship.

Some Bible references for Judas, son of James, include
Matthew 10:1-4
Mark 3:16-19
Luke 6:12-16
Acts 1:12-14

JOHN

(the disciple whom Jesus loved)

John, the brother of James, is one of the three (James, John, and Peter) who were with Jesus at all the special times of Jesus' adult life. John is often thought to be the disciple "whom Jesus loved" (John 13:23). This disciple is not actually named in the Scriptures, but most biblical scholars think that this well-loved disciple was in fact John, the son of Zebedee and the brother of James.

Jesus entrusted his mother, Mary, to John at the foot of the cross (John 19:25-27).

John's shield displays a chalice and serpent. There is a legend that once John was given a cup of poisoned wine to drink. John made the sign of the cross over the chalice and the poison became a serpent and crawled out of the chalice. John is the only disciple other than Thaddeus who escaped a martyr's death. Tradition has it that John lived many years.

Some Bible references for John include
    Matthew 10:1-4
    Mark 1:29; 3:16-19; 9:2; 10:35-45; 13:3-4
    Luke 6:12-16; 8:51
    John 13:23; 19:26-27
    Acts 1:12-14

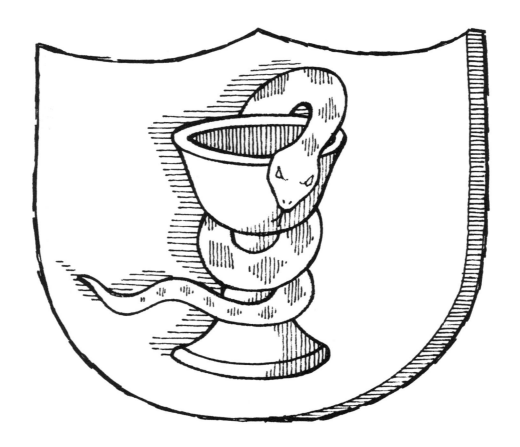

Symbols of Faith

MATTHEW

Matthew appears in every list of the disciples. Matthew was a member of a very hated group, the tax collectors. At the time of Christ, tax collectors were considered to be no better than thieves because they could "add on" to the taxes they collected for their own personal gain. Jesus himself called Matthew to join the disciples. Matthew left his old ways behind and followed Jesus, in the process changing both his own life and the lives of many others. Matthew is considered to be the author of the Gospel According to Matthew.

Matthew's shield displays three moneybags that symbolize his occupation before becoming a disciple.

Some Bible references for Matthew include
   Matthew 9:9-13; 10:1-4
   Mark 3:16-19
   Luke 6:12-16
   Acts 1:12-14

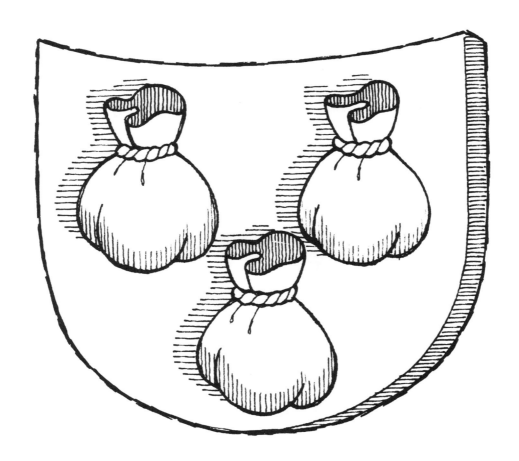

PHILIP

Philip was the first Christian missionary. After Philip was called to discipleship by Jesus, he went and told his friend Nathanael that he had found the one "about whom Moses in the law and also the prophets wrote" (John 1:45).

But Philip is most remembered for saying, "Six months' wages would not buy enough bread for each of them to get a little" (John 6:7). This was in response to Jesus' question about how they were to feed the crowds in the story of the feeding of the five thousand.

Philip's shield displays two loaves of bread and a cross. The bread symbolizes the feeding of the five thousand and the cross symbolizes how Philip faithfully followed Jesus and the way of the cross. It does not symbolize how Philip died.

Some Bible references for Philip include
    Matthew 10:1-4
    Mark 3:16-19
    Luke 6:12-16
    John 1:45
    John 6:7
    Acts 8:4-13

Symbols of Faith

SIMON THE ZEALOT

Very little is known about Simon. He was probably called "the Zealot" because of his political or religious views. (We are not sure which.) There were groups of Jews at the time of Jesus who wanted to be free of Roman rule. These Jews became known as the "Zealots."

Some people feel that since Simon was called "the Zealot" he may have had a rather violent nature that was drawn to Jesus' talk of a "new kingdom," mistaking it for a new *earthly* kingdom, free of the Romans. However, there is no way to be sure how Simon felt.

Simon was also called "the Cananaean"—an early name for the people who later came to be called "Zealots."

Simon's shield displays fish and a book. The fish remind us that Simon was a "fisher of men" and the book is a symbol of the Gospel, the good news of Jesus Christ, which early Christians wrote down on scrolls made of papyrus.

Some Bible references for Simon the Zealot include
    Matthew 10:1-4
    Mark 3:16-19
    Luke 6:12-16
    Acts 1:12-14

THOMAS

We don't know very much about Thomas from the Gospels of Matthew, Mark, or Luke. But in the Gospel of John we find one of the most famous post-Resurrection stories—the story of Thomas asking for proof of Jesus' resurrection that earned Thomas the name "Doubting Thomas."

The name *Thomas* means "twin," but we do not know who his twin was.

Thomas's shield features a carpenter's square and spears. The carpenter's square represents the tradition that Thomas went to India and built a church with his own hands. The spears represent the tradition that Thomas was martyred by being stabbed with a spear.

Some Bible references for Thomas include
    Matthew 10:1-4
    Mark 3:16-19
    Luke 6:12-16
    John 11:16; 14:5; 20:24-29 (the "Doubting Thomas" story); 21:1-14
    Acts 1:12-14

Symbols of Faith

JUDAS ISCARIOT

Judas is a name associated with shame and treachery. Judas Iscariot is the disciple who betrayed Jesus. There is some disagreement among scholars about why exactly Judas betrayed Jesus, but the Bible is very specific about several things: Judas was the treasurer of the group; Judas betrayed Jesus with a kiss and received thirty pieces of silver for it; and Judas hung himself because of what he had done.

Sometimes coins and a rope are shown on Judas's shield, signifying his betrayal of Jesus and his death by hanging. But because of Judas's betrayal of Jesus, the church gave him no official symbol, instead displaying a blank shield.

Some Bible references for Judas Iscariot include
    Matthew 10:1-4; 26:20-25; 27:3-10
    Mark 3:16-19; 14:10-11
    Luke 6:12-16
    John 13:21-30

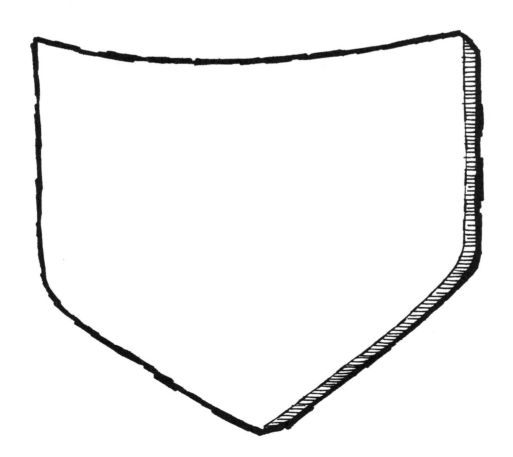

Activity: Disciples Gallery

You will need:

Bibles

crayons, felt-tip markers, pastels, or colored pencils

scissors

index cards

white drawing paper

construction paper

glue

pens

Post photocopies of pages 140 to 151, the descriptions of the disciples and the disciple shields, where everyone can see them. Divide your group into teams, or let everyone work individually. Assign each team (or individual) one of the original twelve disciples (or, if you have fewer than twelve teams, assign two or more disciples as needed).

Ask each team to read the information about their disciple on the posted sheets, look at the shield, and read the Scripture passages associated with their disciple.

Then have everyone use the provided craft materials to make a portrait of their disciple, with a short statement about the disciple on an accompanying index card. The portraits (and statements) can be funny, serious, informative, or descriptive—whatever style they think will help others learn more about the disciples. Encourage creativity. When the portraits are finished, ask everyone to use construction paper to make a frame to go around each portrait. Hang these portraits, along with the index-card statements, where they can easily be seen by others.

Activity: Modern Disciples Gallery

You will need:

instamatic camera and film (or old photos)

art supplies such as felt-tip markers, construction paper, scissors, and glue (optional)

index cards

pens

Create a gallery of the "disciples" that you see every day in your church and community. Divide your group into teams and let each team decide on one or more "modern disciples" to include in the gallery. (This project may take one or two weeks to complete.)

Equip each team with an instamatic camera and send them out to take a picture of the modern disciples they chose, or obtain an old photo of each modern disciple. Ask each team to write a short description on an index card of how the person in their portrait is a modern disciple of Jesus. (Let them decorate the index cards with borders and fancy lettering, if you like, and make construction-paper frames for the Modern Disciples Gallery portraits.) If taking photos or using old pictures is not an option for your group, have your artists draw their own renditions of the modern disciples they are honoring.

Then take pictures, gather photos, or draw portraits of all the members of your group. Be sure to add index cards that describe how these people are acting as modern disciples.

Hang all the portraits in a large room and send out invitations to a showing of your Modern Disciples Gallery. Serve refreshments and make sure everyone takes a tour.

The Jesse Tree

The Christian Year

Jesse Tree

The Jesse Tree is a tree of the symbols that help us focus on the true meaning of Advent, the true preparation for the coming of Christ, and what that really means to us. Some people put one symbol for each day of Advent on the Jesse Tree, which helps maintain the focus on the holiness of the season. Others put just a few symbols on the Jesse Tree as a symbolic representation of Jesus' lineage.

Some people think of the Jesse Tree as Jesus' family tree. After all, the term Jesse Tree *comes from the name of the father of the great king of Israel, King David, Jesse. It is from the line of David (therefore of Jesse) that the Messiah was to come. "A shoot shall come out from the stump of Jesse, and a branch shall grow out of his roots" (Isaiah 11:1).*

Activity: Decorate a Jesse Tree

You will need:
>   list of Jesse Tree symbols on page 156
>   tree and stand
>   craft supplies for making symbol ornaments
>   photocopies of symbol patterns (optional)

The Jesse Tree is often made from a bare tree with no leaves. A dead or dormant tree or large branch set securely in a large bucket of sand works well. However, you can also use any evergreen Christmas tree to make your Jesse Tree since the ornaments are the key to this activity.

You will find that not all of the symbols listed for the Jesse Tree are included in this book. You may want to make just the ornaments for which you have patterns, or you may want to go ahead and use your own methods to make all of the listed Jesse Tree ornaments. Be creative and have fun with the Jesse Tree experience! A few possible ornament-making methods are listed below.

*   Make your Jesse Tree ornaments as "stained glass" miniatures. See page 74 for directions for making paper look like stained glass.

*   Create felt Jesse Tree ornaments (either flat or stuffed) and appliqué them with symbols. See page 60 for appliqué ideas.

*   Shape self-drying clay into Jesse Tree ornaments. Roll the clay out flat and use cookie cutters or knives to cut out ornament-sized pieces (ovals, circles, squares, or other shapes). Then use a pointed stick to "etch" a design onto each ornament. Before the clay dries, be sure to poke a hole at the top of each ornament for hanging. If you'd like, paint designs on the ornaments after they have dried completely.

Symbols of Faith

Jesse Tree Symbols

ALTAR—Zechariah and Elizabeth
ANGEL—angels
APPLE—Adam and Eve
ARK—Noah
CROWN—Solomon
FIVE-POINTED STAR—Bethlehem
HARP—David
HEALING HAND SUPERIMPOSED ON A DESCENDING DOVE—Elisha
LADDER—Jacob
LAMP—Samuel
LILY—Mary
LONG-SLEEVED COAT—Joseph

MANGER or CHI RHO—Birth of Jesus
OPEN BIBLE—Jeremiah
RAM—Isaac
RAVEN—Elijah
ROSE (symbolizes prophecy)—Isaiah
SAW—Joseph the carpenter
SCALLOPED SHELL (without water drops)—John the Baptist
SHEPHERD'S STAFF—shepherds
STONE TABLETS—Moses
STONE WALL—Nehemiah the builder
TENT—Abraham

The Church Year

SEASON	COLOR
Advent	purple or blue
Christmas (Christmas Eve through Epiphany)	white or gold
Season After the Epiphany (Ordinary Time)	green
exceptions are	
first Sunday After the Epiphany (The Lord's Baptism)	white
Last Sunday of Ordinary Time (The Transfiguration)	white
Lent	purple
Holy Week	red
except Holy Thursday, Good Friday, Holy Saturday	no color
Easter Season	white or gold
Day of Pentecost	red
Season After Pentecost (Ordinary Time or Kingdomtide)	green
exceptions are	
First Sunday After Pentecost (Trinity Sunday)	white
All Saints Day	white
Thanksgiving	red or white
Christ the King Sunday	white

Church year seasons and colors adapted from *The United Methodist Book of Worship*, page 224.
Copyright © 1992 The United Methodist Publishing House. Used by permission.

Symbols of Faith

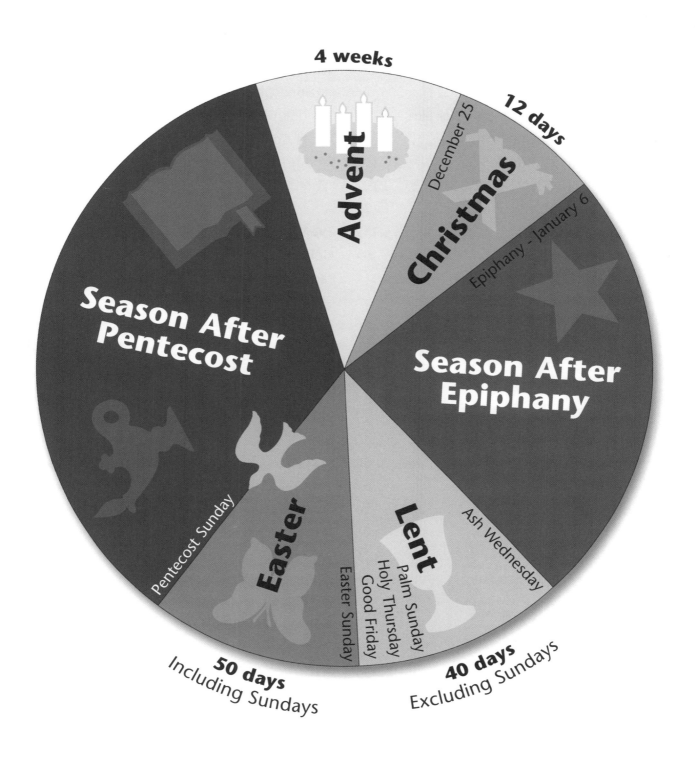

4 weeks

Advent

December 25

12 days

Christmas

Epiphany - January 6

Season After Epiphany

Season After Pentecost

Ash Wednesday

Lent

Palm Sunday
Holy Thursday
Good Friday

Easter Sunday

Easter

Pentecost Sunday

50 days
Including Sundays

40 days
Excluding Sundays

Index of Activities

Symbols of Faith